HUMOROUS PLAYS
for
TEEN-AGERS

CHRISTINA HAMLETT

Publishers   **PLAYS, INC.**   *Boston*

Library of Congress Cataloging-in-Publication Data

Hamlett, Christina.
Humorous plays for teenagers.

Summary: A collection of one-act comedies, melo-dramas, and curtain-raisers; for use in schools, clubs, drama groups, and libraries; and using real-life situations and dialogue.
  1. Children's plays, American.   2. Young adult drama, American. [1. Plays]   I. Title
PS3558.A4446H8 1986   812'.54   86-16916
ISBN 0-8238-0276-0 (pbk.)

Manufactured in Canada

To Dan'l and Louise
   . . . for giving a new kid a break.

Contents

HUMOROUS PLAYS

for

TEEN-AGERS

Hairum-Scarum

Characters

OLIVIA, *owner of the salon*
HILDA, *her assistant*
GOLDILOCKS
RAPUNZEL
CINDERELLA
BRIAR ROSE
ALICE

TIME: *The present.*
SETTING: *The reception area of the Fantastic Frills Salon. Table with phone on it is down left. Three archways leading to "styling booths" are upstage. Main entrance to salon is right. Color scheme is pink and white; photos of different hairstyles adorn the walls. Wig heads, hair spray can, magazines, etc. round out the salon decor.*
AT RISE: OLIVIA *is sitting at table, doing her nails.*

HILDA *enters from one of arches and crosses to* OLIVIA.

OLIVIA *(Sighing heavily):* Hilda, this has to be the slowest day we've ever had!

HILDA: You can say that again.

OLIVIA: I'm almost tempted to close up shop and call it a day.

HILDA: You might as well. *(Indicating archway)* We've styled and restyled each other's hair so much, we're bored to tears back there! *(Phone rings.)*

OLIVIA: Wait a minute! Things could be looking up! *(Answers phone)* Good morning. Fantastic Frills Salon. . . . An appointment this afternoon? *(Smiles at* HILDA*)* Yes, I think we can fit you in. *(Writing in calendar)* Name, please? . . . Helen. . . . Yes, two o'clock would be fine. . . . A special occasion? *(Nodding)* Your face is going to launch a thousand ships so you want to look your best? . . . Don't worry, Helen. We'll send you out in style. O.K., we'll see you at two. *(Hangs up)*

HILDA: Who was that, Olivia?

OLIVIA: Some woman named Helen. She lives in Troy. She said something about looking special for Paris.

HILDA *(Pleased):* Wow! Sounds as if there'll be a big tip in it for us.

OLIVIA: Don't count your curlers before they're in. *(*GOLDILOCKS *runs in right, quite breathless and looking behind her as if being pursued.)*

GOLDILOCKS: Is this the Fantastic Frills Salon?

HILDA: At your service. I'm Hilda, and this is Olivia, the owner.

OLIVIA: What can we do for you, Miss. . . . ?

GOLDILOCKS: Locks. Goldi Locks. And what you can do is get me out of a lot of hot water!

HILDA: What's the problem?

GOLDILOCKS: Well, there are three bears—a father, a mother, and a baby bear who whines all the time.

HILDA: What about them?

GOLDILOCKS: It seems they've got a warrant out for my arrest.

OLIVIA: *Arrest?*

HILDA: I don't like the sound of this, Olivia.

GOLDILOCKS *(Reassuring them):* Listen, it's nothing serious, really. I wandered into their house by mistake and they got in a big huff about it. I tried to explain, but would they listen? Of course not! In fact, they were downright grizzly about it and told the police I broke their chairs and ate their food, and—

OLIVIA *(Interrupting):* I'm confused. What is it that you want us to do?

GOLDILOCKS *(Indicating her hair):* Well, see this hair?

HILDA: Yes, it's very pretty.

OLIVIA: Lovely.

GOLDILOCKS: It's also a dead giveaway. They're looking for a girl with golden locks. Until I can get a good attorney to defend me, I need a disguise. Something brunette, maybe. Straight, with feathered bangs.

OLIVIA: Well—

HILDA: She really does seem like a sweet girl, Olivia.

GOLDILOCKS: Will you do it? Please?

OLIVIA: Oh, all right. (*To* HILDA) Take her back to Gladys.

HILDA: Will do.

OLIVIA (*To* GOLDILOCKS): You'll be a different person when we see you again.

GOLDILOCKS (*As she exits with* HILDA): Thanks! You're a real lifesaver! (*They exit. Phone rings.*)

OLIVIA (*Into phone*): Good morning. Fantastic Frills Salon. (*Listens in amazement*) What? . . . Why, that's terrible! . . . It completely turned to gold? . . . The brush, too? (*Shakes her head, as* HILDA *returns*) I've never heard of anything like that happening before! . . . Well, you might try a good conditioner first, and, if that doesn't work, we'll make an appointment for you. . . . Good luck. (*Hangs up*)

HILDA: What was that all about?

OLIVIA: It's the most bizarre story I've ever heard. It seems that when this girl's father touched things, they turned to gold, just like that! (*Waves hand*) Anyway, he offered to brush her hair and as he touched it—zap! Instant gold—and the brush along with it!

HILDA: That's the weirdest thing I've ever heard in my life.

RAPUNZEL *(Calling from offstage):* Yoo-hoo! Anybody there?

OLIVIA *(Waving, as if to someone in main doorway):* Come on in—we're open! (RAPUNZEL *enters; she has long hair that drags on the floor.*)

RAPUNZEL: Thank goodness. *(Trips over hair)* I've been tripping all over the street, looking for a salon that's open.

HILDA: My goodness! Look at that hair, Olivia!

RAPUNZEL: Yes, that's what I'm here for. I want you to cut it.

OLIVIA: But it's absolutely gorgeous! Why on earth would you want to cut it?

RAPUNZEL: You'd want it cut, too, if you knew the trouble it's caused me.

HILDA: Like what?

RAPUNZEL: Like having a witch keep me locked up in a huge tower without an elevator.

OLIVIA: If it doesn't have an elevator, how does anybody get to the top?

RAPUNZEL *(Pointing to hair):* Three guesses and the first two don't count.

HILDA: By climbing up your hair?

RAPUNZEL: Bingo. *(Shakes head)* Talk about a headache.

OLIVIA: That's incredible.

RAPUNZEL: I mean, here I am, doing my nails or watching the soaps, and I have to listen to

"Rapunzel, Rapunzel, let down your hair," day in and day out. I'm sick of it. I want one of those cute short styles. I think they're really me!

OLIVIA: Well . . . if you're really sure.

RAPUNZEL: Believe me—I'm sure.

OLIVIA (*To* HILDA): Take her to Loretta—she loves to cut hair.

HILDA: We're on our way. (*Exits with* RAPUNZEL. *Phone rings.* OLIVIA *answers it.*)

OLIVIA (*Into phone*): Good morning, Fantastic Frills Salon. (*Listens*) Yes, that sounds pretty messy. . . . Of course, I'd be startled, too. A spider, you say? . . . Oh, dear. (HILDA *re-enters.*) You might try a good shampoo and give us a call if all of it doesn't come out. . . . Certainly, any time. (*Hangs up*)

HILDA: Another customer?

OLIVIA: One of Esther's regulars—that Muffet girl who's into health foods.

HILDA: Remember that stuff she was eating last week—curds and whey? Ich!

OLIVIA: Yes. I guess she was outside, eating some of that awful concoction, and a spider scared her so much, she jumped and got a whole bowl full of it on her head.

HILDA: Serves her right for eating it in the first place. (CINDERELLA *enters. She wears ragged clothes and one shoe, which appears to be made of glass.*)

CINDERELLA: Pardon me, but can I get an appointment this morning?

OLIVIA: Of course! Come on in.

CINDERELLA: Thanks. Listen, I'm in a hurry—my stepmother and stepsisters will be back right after lunch and I have to get home and clean the fireplace before they get there.

HILDA: Forgive me for staring, but did you know you're wearing only one shoe?

CINDERELLA: Of course! I lost it the other night at a discotheque.

OLIVIA: How could you lose a shoe at a discotheque?

CINDERELLA: Well, at the time, I was preoccupied. There was this really handsome guy who turned out to be a prince or something. And then I had to watch the time or else I'd be stuck with mice and pumpkins out in the parking lot and no way to get home. (OLIVIA *and* HILDA *exchange looks.*) Anyway, I want to look really fantastic this afternoon, because this guy may be paying me a visit.

HILDA: How nice!

CINDERELLA: Yes, especially if it fits.

OLIVIA: If what fits?

CINDERELLA: The shoe he found—the mate to this one. If it does, I can leave this life of drudgery behind and waltz off in grand style.

HILDA: I see.

OLIVIA (*Looking at calendar*): Francine just happens to have an opening. Hilda will show you the way.

CINDERELLA: Terrific. (*Starting to exit*) By the way, if the shoe fits, I'll see that you get an invitation to the wedding, O.K.?

OLIVIA: Wonderful. (CINDERELLA *and* HILDA *exit. A moment later,* HILDA *re-enters, followed shortly by* BRIAR ROSE, *whose hair is a tangled mass, with curls tied in different colored ribbons.*)

BRIAR ROSE: Hi, there!

HILDA *(Gasping):* Oh, no!

BRIAR ROSE *(Puzzled):* Oh, no?

HILDA: Your hair. Olivia—look at that!

OLIVIA: I haven't seen a hairstyle like that since— goodness, but I can't even remember!

HILDA: You're here for an appointment, I hope?

BRIAR ROSE: Yes, if you have one available on short notice . . .

OLIVIA: Forgive us for appearing rude, but where have you been for the last hundred years?

BRIAR ROSE: Actually, I've been asleep.

HILDA: You must be the one they call Sleeping Beauty.

BRIAR ROSE: Yes. You see, the last thing I remember was pricking my finger on a spinning wheel and falling into a deep sleep. Next thing I knew, this strange man I had never seen before gave me a kiss and woke me up.

OLIVIA *(Skeptically):* So you've been asleep for a hundred years?

HILDA *(Sarcastically):* That explains the hairstyle, all right.

BRIAR ROSE: Is something wrong?

OLIVIA: Yes, dear, your hairstyle. No one has worn

it that way for decades. Or, in your case, centuries. But don't worry, Hilda's going to take you back to Martha—she's a whiz with the new styles. (HILDA *and* BRIAR ROSE *exit*.)

ALICE *(Entering):* Am I late? *(Her blond hair is quite disheveled).*

OLIVIA: Late for what?

ALICE: For a very important date.

OLIVIA: Do you have an appointment?

ALICE: Oh dear, I just can't seem to recall. My life has been rather turbulent lately. And it's all because of that silly rabbit!

OLIVIA: What rabbit?

ALICE: The one with the waistcoat and pocketwatch that I followed down the rabbit hole. It was infinitely more interesting, you see, than being read to by my sister from a book without any pictures. Books without pictures are so boring, you know.

OLIVIA: I suppose. But about the rabbit?

ALICE: Well, he led me on a wild goose chase . . . or rather, a wild rabbit chase all over the countryside. That's the last time I'll ever do that, believe me!

OLIVIA: Excuse me, but your hair—

ALICE: Is a mess! Tell me about it! The way my afternoon went yesterday, I'm lucky I still have my head! It was bad enough eating those mushrooms and playing trivial pursuit about ravens and writing desks at the tea party, but when the Red Queen started shouting "Off with her head—"

Well, I've had quite a day.

OLIVIA: Yes, I imagine. But back to the subject at hand—

ALICE: Which is?

OLIVIA: The reason you came in here. Did you want an appointment?

ALICE: An appointment? Of course not. I'm still trying to catch up with that rabbit. I could have sworn he came in here.

OLIVIA *(Looking around):* But where could he have gone?

ALICE: Aha! *(Pointing at something off left)* There he is . . . and here I go! *(Crossing quickly)*

OLIVIA: Go where?

ALICE: Through the looking glass—where else? *(Exits left; GOLDILOCKS re-enters, wearing wig of long, black, straight hair.)*

GOLDILOCKS: You guys are fantastic! I love it!

OLIVIA: Leaving so soon?

GOLDILOCKS *(Checking watch):* Yes, the porridge should have cooled down by now. Thanks! *(Exits; RAPUNZEL re-enters, with a short, sleek hairdo.)*

RAPUNZEL: Wow! I feel 50 pounds lighter already!

OLIVIA: Can I offer you some coffee before you leave?

RAPUNZEL *(Romantically):* Thanks, but no. I've got a date with a wonderful guy I met the other day while I was hanging my hair out the window to dry. *(Exits; CINDERELLA enters; she has a new hairdo.)*

CINDERELLA: My fairy godmother was right—you do work miracles here!

OLIVIA: Your hair is beautiful!

CINDERELLA: The folks at home are going to turn absolutely green with envy! *(Exits.* BRIAR ROSE *enters, wearing multi-colored punk-style wig.)*

BRIAR ROSE: How do you like the new me?

OLIVIA *(Startled):* Briar Rose! For a second I didn't recognize you!

BRIAR ROSE: Pretty chic, eh?

OLIVIA: Think you'll become one of our regulars?

BRIAR ROSE: Sure, why not?

OLIVIA: Just don't wait another hundred years! (BRIAR ROSE *laughs and exits.* HILDA *re-enters.)*

HILDA: Where did everybody go?

OLIVIA: They're off to turn people's heads, I guess.

HILDA: Gee—it sure is quiet again, isn't it?

OLIVIA: Yes, well, you know what they say, Hilda.

HILDA: What's that?

OLIVIA: Hair today and gone tomorrow. *(Curtain)*

THE END

PRODUCTION NOTES

HAIRUM-SCARUM

Characters: 7 female.

Playing Time: 15 minutes.

Costumes: Olivia and Hilda wear everyday clothing; others are dressed like the fairy tale characters, with appropriate wigs for changing hairstyles.

Properties: Calendar; hair-care knick-knacks.

Setting: Reception area of the Fantastic Frills Salon. Table with phone on it is down left. Three archways leading to "styling booths" are upstage. Main entrance to salon is right. Color scheme is pink and white; photos of different hairstyles adorn the walls. Wig heads, hair spray can, magazines, etc. round out the decor.

Sound and Lighting: No special effects.

When Pirates Ruled the Sea

Characters

CAPTAIN
BOSUN COLLINS
ROGER JOLLY
LILLIAN
THE COUNTESS

TIME: *When pirates ruled the ocean.*
SETTING: *Captain's private quarters on board* The
Scarlet Raven. *Large desk, covered with maps,
papers, etc., and chair are center. Glove with
hook, tankard, eye patch, pirate hat, and tele-
scope are lying on desk. Two crates right marked*
RUM *and* ALE *serve as table. Backdrop shows
portholes in wooden wall.*
AT RISE: CAPTAIN, *wearing glasses, is seated at*

desk, hunched over maps. He squints, shakes head, then after a moment turns one map upside down, looks quizzically at it. Finally, in annoyance, he drops maps on floor, then looks up and notices audience. With a chuckle, he stands, removes glasses and places them carefully on desk.

CAPTAIN *(To audience):* You're probably sitting there asking yourselves how I got into this situation in the first place. *(With sweeping gesture)* What am I doing as the captain of *(Ominously)* the *Scarlet Raven*, a pirate ship whose very name strikes terror in the hearts of seasoned sailors? *(Sighs)* Well, it's a long story. *(Pacing)* It all started before I was born, an incidental observation that absolves me from the nefarious practices into which, as an adult, I was later thrust. *(Smiling)* My father was a gambler. *(Dryly)* Unfortunately, games of chance were not his strong suit. He was down to his last doubloon when the Count of Bella Donna made him a most unusual proposition: He could win back all of his losses, or turn over his first-born son to the Count when such son reached majority. *(After a pause)* Now, my father thought this was a very shrewd venture to undertake, considering that my mother had blessed him with six daughters, with a seventh on the way. *(Dramatically)* He boldly placed the wager *(Shrugs)*, and lost almost immediately. My mother, naturally, was not thrilled with his announcement upon his return home six months later, especially in light of the joyous announcement of her own. *(Brightening)* The good news, of course, was that I didn't become the Count's indentured servant as I had dreaded all along that I would. . . . The bad news is that I was betrothed to his elder daughter, sight unseen. Her name, not inappropriately, was Flotilla. *(Sighs)* Pleasingly plump, her father described her . . . translated to mean that, if the ships in the Spanish Armada had used her for cover, they could have escaped the British before anyone noticed they were missing. *(Knocking is heard.* CAPTAIN *calls off.)* Who goes there?

COLLINS *(Offstage):* Bosun Collins, Cap'n.

CAPTAIN *(To audience):* Maybe if I ignore him, he'll go away. *(Continues his story)* As I was saying— *(Knocking interrupts him. He shrugs.)* Then again, maybe not. *(Calls off)* What do you want? I'm busy now.

COLLINS: It's life and death, Cap'n.

CAPTAIN *(To audience):* Do you sense an element of urgency here? Then again, it could be a clever ruse to expose the secret I was just about to tell you. *(Sighs heavily)* I may as well let him in. *(Calls off)* Just a minute, Collins. (CAPTAIN *crosses to table, puts on eye patch, hat, then glove with attached hook. He opens door, and* COLLINS *enters.)* Well, Collins, get on with it. What's so urgent?

COLLINS: Would I be disturbin' you, Cap'n?

CAPTAIN *(Firmly):* As a matter of fact, you are. *(Takes pistol from belt)* And you know how I hate *(Cocks gun)* to be disturbed.

COLLINS *(Nervously):* Aye, Cap'n.

CAPTAIN: I suggest you be quick about it.

COLLINS *(Carefully):* 'Tis a storm off starboard, Cap'n.

CAPTAIN *(Musing):* Hm-m-m. Starboard. *(Then, in annoyed tone)* Well, what do you want me to do about it?

COLLINS: I thought you'd be wantin' to change course to steer clear of her, Cap'n.

CAPTAIN *(Pacing past* COLLINS*):* Yes. Excellent idea, Bosun. I was just thinking of that myself. *(With casual wave of his hook)* Take care of it, will you? *(After a pause, turns to face* COLLINS*)* Well? What are you waiting for?

COLLINS *(Snidely):* Your orders, Cap'n.

CAPTAIN *(Tucking gun back into belt):* Oh, I leave it to your discretion, Bosun.

COLLINS: My discretion, Cap'n?

CAPTAIN: Hands-on training. It's a new concept that's all the rage in Verona. *(Turning away from* COLLINS, *he picks up spyglass on table and looks through the wrong end.)* Whatever you think is best for the ship.

COLLINS *(Withdrawing dagger from belt):* Aye, Cap'n. *(Raising dagger, he starts to lunge at* CAPTAIN.*)* What's best for the ship. *(Knocking is* *heard.* COLLINS *freezes in lunging position, dagger raised.)*

CAPTAIN *(Annoyed, as he turns):* Oh, bother. *(Notices* COLLINS)

COLLINS *(Displaying dagger; smiling):* A gift from my mother, Cap'n.

CAPTAIN *(Not convinced):* Yes, well put it away before you hurt someone. *(Knocking is heard again.* CAPTAIN *calls off.)* Who goes there?

ROGER *(Offstage):* Roger Jolly, Cap'n.

CAPTAIN (*To* COLLINS): Uh—see to the storm, will you, Bosun?

COLLINS *(Putting dagger back into belt):* Aye, Cap'n. *(Exits left)*

CAPTAIN *(To audience):* There's something about that man I just don't trust. *(Knocking again)* Enter!

ROGER *(Entering):* You sent for me, Cap'n?

CAPTAIN: I did? When?

ROGER: Just now, Cap'n.

CAPTAIN *(Puzzled):* No, I said you could come in, but I didn't send for you.

ROGER: Are you sure?

CAPTAIN: Of course I'm sure.

ROGER *(After a moment):* Were you *going* to send for me, then? Perhaps I'm early.

CAPTAIN: Not that I know of.

ROGER: Oh. *(After a moment, breaking into a grin)* Well, as long as I'm here, is there anything you'd be needin' me to do, Cap'n?

CAPTAIN *(Shaking head):* Can't think of anything.

ROGER: Not a thing? A deck to swab? A tankard of ale to replenish?

CAPTAIN *(Mildly amazed):* You're certainly a helpful chap, Roger.

ROGER: Aye, Cap'n. (CAPTAIN *crosses to desk and puts foot up on chair. ROGER follows CAPTAIN, whips out a handkerchief, and proceeds to buff CAPTAIN's boots.*)

CAPTAIN: You know, Roger, I get the distinct feeling the rest of the crew dislikes me.

ROGER: Aye, Cap'n . . . but then, they'd sell their own mothers' souls to the devil.

CAPTAIN: What about you, Roger?

ROGER: I'm an orphan, Cap'n.

CAPTAIN *(Confidentially):* What are they thinking, Roger?

ROGER *(Confidentially):* They're revolting, Cap'n.

CAPTAIN: I *know* they're revolting, but what are they *thinking*?

ROGER: I am loyal to your command, Cap'n. (CAPTAIN *turns away. ROGER takes vial from his pocket as he talks.*) As loyal as the day is long.

CAPTAIN (*Flattered, but still not looking at* ROGER): Thank you. That's nice to know.

ROGER *(As he empties contents of vial into tankard on desk):* 'Tis many a captain I've sailed with, but never one like you to command my respect.

CAPTAIN: Thank you again. But what I'd really like to know—

ROGER *(Interrupting):* If there's a single man on board to be trusted, Cap'n—*(Putting vial back into pocket)* it's Roger Jolly.

CAPTAIN *(Looking at* ROGER): I'll remember that when promotions come up.

ROGER *(Handing tankard to* CAPTAIN): To your health, Cap'n.

CAPTAIN *(Starting to take it with hook, then using other hand):* And to yours. Uh—will you join me?

ROGER *(Proudly):* Not while on duty, Cap'n.

CAPTAIN: Good man. (ROGER *watches him.*) That will be all, Roger.

ROGER: Aye, Cap'n. *(As he exits, he looks back at* CAPTAIN, *who raises tankard to* ROGER, *as if in toast. Exits)*

CAPTAIN *(To audience):* As I started to tell you *(Sets tankard down and proceeds to take off glove with hook)*—the date of my nuptials to Miss Flotilla drew near. And so I took the only course of action logical for an intelligent gentleman. I ran away. *(Picks up tankard)* My ship was barely out of port when we were attacked by pirates—by Captain Sebastien, to be specific. *(Reflecting)* Looking back, I realize it was only because of my uncommon and uncanny resemblance to the ruggedly handsome Captain that I was spared a fatefully short walk off the end of the plank. *(Shrugs)* I had assumed, of course, that his suggestion of trading identities was nothing more than a whimsical diversion to pass an afternoon.

When I discovered to my amazement that he had somehow escaped, and that I was stuck with this charade—*(As he lifts tankard to his lips, knocking is heard.* CAPTAIN *calls off.)* Come in! *(Hastily puts tankard down, and puts glove with hook on wrong arm)*

COLLINS *(Entering):* Request permission to report, Cap'n.

CAPTAIN: Proceed, Collins.

COLLINS: I want to discuss the prisoners with you, Cap'n.

CAPTAIN *(Puzzled):* What prisoners?

COLLINS: Prisoners from *The Cotillion,* Cap'n. The ship we took at dawn.

CAPTAIN *(Annoyed):* By whose orders?

COLLINS *(Slyly):* Would you be contradictin' your own orders, Cap'n?

CAPTAIN: *I* gave those orders?

COLLINS: Would you be havin' the prisoners walk the plank before or after?

CAPTAIN: Before or after what?

COLLINS: The storm, Cap'n.

CAPTAIN: Well, as long as we've plenty of room on the ship, we can put them up until the storm breaks, and then find some place to drop them off.

COLLINS *(Snidely):* I suppose next you'll be wantin' to return the loot.

CAPTAIN: The loot?

COLLINS: It was a weddin' party we plundered, Cap'n.

CAPTAIN *(Suspiciously):* A wedding party? Collins, what was the name of the ship you boarded?

COLLINS: *The Cotillion*, Cap'n.

CAPTAIN: *The Cotillion* out of Lisbon?

COLLINS: Aye, Cap'n. We glimpsed the Portuguese flag before the ship went under.

CAPTAIN *(Slowly):* Were there any ladies on board?

COLLINS: Aye, Cap'n.

CAPTAIN *(Cautiously):* An older one, and a . . . pleasingly plump one, perhaps?

COLLINS: Aye, there was an older one, Cap'n. But the other—*(Smiles)* well, she was pleasant, all right.

CAPTAIN: Hm-m-m.

COLLINS: Would ye be wantin' to look the wenches over, Cap'n?

CAPTAIN: Yes, I suppose so. (COLLINS *is looking quizzically at* CAPTAIN.) Is something wrong, Bosun?

COLLINS *(Pointing):* What's the matter with your arm?

CAPTAIN *(Looking down and realizing hook is askew):* Nothing. Nothing at all. *(Brusquely)* Now, carry on!

COLLINS: Aye, Cap'n. *(Exits.* CAPTAIN *takes off glove with hook, tossing it onto desk.)*

CAPTAIN: What have I gotten myself into? *(Lifts eye patch)* And more important, how do I get myself out of it? *(Pacing)* What an extraordinary circumstance that *The Cotillion* is the very ship on which

Flotilla and her mother had booked their passage. *(Sighs)* How narrowly one sometimes escapes disaster! *(Pause)* Speaking of escape, of course, I should be plotting my own before I'm interrupted again. *(Crosses to desk, puts on glasses and begins rummaging through papers and maps as* ROGER *enters, carrying a large box.* CAPTAIN *looks up, and with a start quickly pulls his eye patch down over his glasses, and puts both hands behind his back.)* Roger! I didn't hear you knock.

ROGER *(Quickly):* Not having a free hand, Cap'n, I—

CAPTAIN *(Suspiciously):* What do you have in the box?

ROGER: Rummage, Cap'n. I was just tidying up.

CAPTAIN: Yes, well, I'd appreciate it if you'd do your tidying elsewhere. I'm busy just now.

ROGER: Aye, Cap'n. *(Staring at* CAPTAIN)

CAPTAIN: Is something wrong?

ROGER *(Quickly):* No, Cap'n. Nothing at all. *(Turning to exit, then looking back)* Would you like a fresh tankard of ale, Cap'n? Was the last too weak a draught?

CAPTAIN *(Looking into tankard):* No, I haven't finished what I have here. And it's quite fine, thank you.

ROGER: Aye, Cap'n. *(Exits.* CAPTAIN *removes his glasses, puts patch over eye and glove with hook on wrong arm.* COLLINS *enters with* LILLIAN *and* COUNTESS, *both wearing long dresses.* COUNTESS *is heavily made up.* COLLINS *addresses* CAP-

TAIN.) These are the wenches, Cap'n.

COUNTESS *(Imperiously):* Wenches, indeed!

LILLIAN *(Flirtatiously):* So, you're the Captain?

COUNTESS *(Quickly):* You're speaking out of turn, dear. A most undesirable trait in young women.

LILLIAN *(Shrugging):* I was just curious.

COUNTESS: Well, of course he's the Captain. *(Disdainfully)* The one who never taught all of these hoodlums their manners.

CAPTAIN: If you'll just allow me to . . . (COUNTESS *approaches him in overbearing way. He draws back.)*

COUNTESS: When my husband hears about this, he'll have you tossed to the sharks.

LILLIAN: Oh, really, Mother. How silly.

COUNTESS *(To* LILLIAN*):* I told your father we should have taken another ship, but does he ever listen to me? *(Mimicking)* "No," he said, "we need the money for the wedding. Do you know what this is costing me already?" *(Pause)* Really, he can be so petty. We couldn't go on a *safe* ship, one with nice accommodations like *The Regency.* No, *we* have to take one that gets captured in the middle of nowhere by pirates. And in addition, they've probably lost our luggage.

CAPTAIN: Madam, please!

COUNTESS *(Sharply):* Don't "Madam" me, young man.

COLLINS *(Taking out his dagger):* Would you like me to take out this one's tongue, Cap'n? *(Holds dagger poised for attack)*

COUNTESS: My tongue?

LILLIAN: I think he means to be quiet, Mother.

CAPTAIN: Yes, please, I need to be able to hear myself think. Now, madam, if you'll just allow me to introduce myself . . .

COUNTESS: You already have. You're the leader of these uncouth ruffians.

COLLINS: You're in the presence of Captain Sebastien.

LILLIAN *(Impressed): The* Captain Sebastien?

CAPTAIN *(Flattered):* You mean you've heard of him? I mean—of me?

LILLIAN: Hasn't everyone?

COUNTESS *(Indignantly):* I've never heard of him, Lillian. How could *you* have heard of him?

LILLIAN: The *Gazette*, Mother. I do read, you know.

COUNTESS *(Annoyed):* What your sister did was bad enough. But for a young woman like you to be educating herself behind her mother's back is totally inexcusable.

CAPTAIN *(To* LILLIAN): What have you read about me?

LILLIAN *(Strolling toward him):* That you're the most ruthless, bloodthirsty, cold-blooded and exciting man on the Seven Seas.

COUNTESS: How many times have I told you that you shouldn't believe the things they write in the tabloids? I absolutely forbid you to engage this dreadful man in further conversation.

LILLIAN: I find him charming. *(During following*

conversation, CAPTAIN *gets hook caught on clothes, and struggles to free it.)*

COUNTESS (*To* CAPTAIN): Now then, Captain Sebastien, if you'll be good enough to let us return to our ship . . .

COLLINS *(Noticing* CAPTAIN'*s struggle):* Need a hand, Cap'n?

CAPTAIN: Very funny, Collins. *(Gets loose)* As you were saying, ladies?

COUNTESS: We wish to be returned to *The Cotillion* at once.

CAPTAIN: I'm afraid that's impossible.

LILLIAN: Why?

COLLINS: Because *The Cotillion* is at the bottom of the ocean . . . where you'll be seein' it soon yourself, if you get my drift.

COUNTESS: What a cruel man!

CAPTAIN: That'll be all, Collins.

COLLINS: Would you have me return the wenches to the hold, Cap'n?

COUNTESS *(Huffily):* Just wait till my husband the Count hears about this!

CAPTAIN: Excuse me, did you say "Count"?

COUNTESS: I most certainly did. *(Proudly)* I am the Countess Angelina de Rosa Amoretta Marie Tarantella—

CAPTAIN: Nice to meet you.

COUNTESS *(Continuing):*—Vicente alla Gina Maletti Gilardi de Bella Donna.

LILLIAN *(Wryly):* Mother doesn't believe in short

introductions, Captain Sebastien.

CAPTAIN: Did you say Bella Donna at the end of all that?

COUNTESS: Yes.

LILLIAN: And I'm—

COUNTESS *(Interrupting her):* He doesn't want to know who you are. Remember that you're be-trothed to a nice young man who will be very upset when he hears about this.

LILLIAN *(Angrily):* A man that Daddy won in a card game.

CAPTAIN *(To audience):* Are you thinking the same thing I am? *(To* COUNTESS*)* If you will allow me, Countess, I should like to speak to your daughter privately.

LILLIAN *(Smiling):* How exciting!

COUNTESS *(Vexed):* I cannot permit this.

CAPTAIN: Bosun. (COLLINS *steps forward, clamps his hand over* COUNTESS's *mouth, and pulls her offstage.*)

LILLIAN *(Watching this, then sighing):* If only it were that easy at home.

CAPTAIN *(Awkwardly):* Uh—would you care for some ale?

LILLIAN: Why, yes, thank you. (CAPTAIN *crosses to table, picks up tankard and hands it to* LILLIAN.*)*

CAPTAIN: Now, tell me about your fiancé.

LILLIAN: There's nothing to tell. We have never even met.

CAPTAIN *(To audience):* The plot thickens. *(To*

LILLIAN) You have never met him?

LILLIAN: No. *(About to take sip, then speaking)* But I am sure I shall be disappointed.

CAPTAIN: How so?

LILLIAN: I hear that he leads a most dull existence in which nothing adventurous ever happens.

CAPTAIN: And the young man's name?

LILLIAN: Thaddeus Lord.

CAPTAIN *(To audience):* Perhaps my flight from matrimonial obligation was premature. *(To* LILLIAN) There is something I must confess.

LILLIAN *(Puzzled):* What's that, sir?

CAPTAIN: First I wish you to tell me your name.

LILLIAN: It's Lillian.

CAPTAIN *(Astonished):* What? You mean, it isn't Flotilla?

LILLIAN: No. Why should it be?

CAPTAIN *(Grasping for an answer):* Because it is a lovely name . . . one that brings a lovely image to mind. Are you sure it's not a pet name called you by your parents?

LILLIAN: Of course not. For it is the name of my elder sister.

CAPTAIN *(In realization):* Oh! I see.

LILLIAN: Mother, needless to say, is most annoyed with her.

CAPTAIN *(Dryly):* Then again, your mother seems easily annoyed.

LILLIAN: Ah—but this is scandalous.

CAPTAIN: Really?

LILLIAN *(Handing tankard to him):* May I confide in you?

CAPTAIN: Of course.

LILLIAN *(Explaining):* My mother and I were to accompany my sister Flotilla to her fiancé's villa. We had barely left port when we discovered that my sister—who had feigned a headache on boarding—was not on the ship at all!

CAPTAIN: Where was she?

LILLIAN: A note pinned to her pillow revealed that she had run off with another man!

CAPTAIN: Shameful! *(Concerned)* Was she never found and brought back home?

LILLIAN *(Dramatically):* I suspect we shall never see her again.

CAPTAIN *(Feigning shock):* What a dilemma!

LILLIAN: And what a scandal! To save face, Mother insisted that *I* pretend to be Master Lord's innocent bride.

CAPTAIN *(Pleased):* What a wonderfully clever idea!

LILLIAN *(Dismayed):* I think it's *dreadful*.

CAPTAIN: But I'm sure you'll find Master Lord to be a wonderful, congenial and upstanding young man, not to mention ruggedly handsome, virtuous and modest.

LILLIAN: He may well be all those things, Captain, but I should like to choose my *own* husband . . . and preferably a rogue who will prove a challenge for me to reform. *(Pause)* Do you happen to know anyone like that?

CAPTAIN *(Slyly):* Perhaps I do.

LILLIAN *(Eagerly):* Who?

CAPTAIN: Well—

LILLIAN *(Suddenly):* But first, tell me your secret.

CAPTAIN: My secret?

LILLIAN: The one you wished to confess.

CAPTAIN: Ah, yes. *(He hands her the tankard and, after a moment, dramatically removes eye patch.)* Ta-da!

LILLIAN *(Puzzled):* That is your secret? That you have two good eyes instead of one?

CAPTAIN: All the better to gaze on you, my dear.

LILLIAN: Anything else? *(After a moment,* CAPTAIN *removes glove with hook and tosses it on desk.)* And that you have two strong arms?

CAPTAIN: The better to hold you with.

LILLIAN *(Amazed):* Is this the extent of your mystery, sir? Or have you other secrets to reveal?

CAPTAIN *(Crossing to her):* We shall discover further secrets together. *(Kisses her)*

LILLIAN: Oh, my! I have never felt this way. (ROGER *sneaks in behind her; he carries a small vial.)*

CAPTAIN: Nor I.

LILLIAN: Can it be love, my bold Captain? (COLLINS *sneaks in behind* CAPTAIN, *carrying pistol.)*

CAPTAIN: It can be nothing else, lovely lady.

LILLIAN: When I look into your eyes, I see no one else.

CAPTAIN *(Fondly):* Nor I.

LILLIAN: Except for the man sneaking up on you.

(CAPTAIN *turns and sees* COLLINS. CAPTAIN *and* LILLIAN *duck, and* COLLINS *shoots* ROGER, *who falls to ground.*)

CAPTAIN *(In amazement):* Collins!

COLLINS *(Hastily, in excuse):* It was Roger's intention from the start to kill you, Cap'n. It's your good fortune that I happened along.

CAPTAIN *(Suspiciously):* And what of your own ambition, Collins?

COLLINS: Was there ever a doubt that I am loyal to your command, Cap'n?

CAPTAIN *(Taking tankard from* LILLIAN): Well, then, Collins—to your health. *(Hands tankard to* COLLINS)

COLLINS: Aye, Cap'n. *(Drinks)*

CAPTAIN *(Glancing at* ROGER'S *body):* Yet he carries no weapon. *(To* COLLINS) How did he intend to kill me?

COLLINS: Poison, Cap'n. *(Looks at tankard, shakes head)*

CAPTAIN: Interesting. (COLLINS *collapses;* CAPTAIN *shrugs and turns back to* LILLIAN, *embraces her.)* Where were we?

COUNTESS *(Running in):* Lillian! I—*(Sees them in embrace)* Well, look at this! I turn my back for five minutes, and what do you do?

LILLIAN *(Surprised):* Mother! You escaped!

COUNTESS: And none too soon. We're about to be attacked. We are surrounded by ships. *(To* CAP-

TAIN) You're in big trouble . . . and get your hands off my daughter!

CAPTAIN: What ships are you talking about?

COUNTESS *(Proudly):* British ships. They've come to rescue us—and to hang you.

LILLIAN: But we've only just found each other!

CAPTAIN: Our romance, it seems, is not destined to run smoothly.

COUNTESS: Come, Lillian. We have to go on deck to be rescued. *(Exits)*

CAPTAIN *(Patting* LILLIAN's *hand as she tears herself away):* Don't despair, Lillian. I'll think of something.

COUNTESS *(Offstage):* Lillian!

LILLIAN *(Suddenly):* Wait! Why don't you pretend to be my fiancé?

CAPTAIN: For what purpose?

LILLIAN: Why, to save your life, of course!

CAPTAIN: Yes—but how?

LILLIAN *(Plotting):* I shall tell our rescuers a passionately moving, and thoroughly convincing, story—that you were captured with us!

CAPTAIN: But what will your mother say?

LILLIAN *(Continuing):* We'll say that she was hit on the head and doesn't remember you. Or else that she *does* remember you and seeks to thwart our star-crossed affair. *(Smiling)* And then, when they are convinced, we shall ask to be married at once by the British captain.

CAPTAIN: A brilliant plan, Lillian!

LILLIAN *(Sighing):* Except, of course, for the lack of proof.

CAPTAIN: Proof of what?

LILLIAN: Your identity. *(Wistfully)* If only there were papers to be found, then all should be taken as the truth. (CAPTAIN *crosses over to desk.)*

CAPTAIN: Maybe—just maybe . . .

LILLIAN: Maybe what?

CAPTAIN *(Rummaging through papers):* What was the name of your young man?

LILLIAN: Thaddeus Lord.

CAPTAIN *(Dramatically unfolding a piece of paper):* What an amazing coincidence, Lillian!

LILLIAN: What is that?

CAPTAIN: Just yesterday we seized a ship, and on that ship was a man with the very name of your sister's fiancé!

LILLIAN: How unusual!

CAPTAIN: Yes, isn't it?

LILLIAN: But what became of the young man?

CAPTAIN: Let us not speak of distressing things, Lillian, when our future is so close at hand. *(Crossing back to her)*

LILLIAN: You do not mind assuming the identity of another?

CAPTAIN *(Dramatically):* My past is already forgotten. How clever you are, Lillian!

LILLIAN: And how in love!

CAPTAIN *(With arms outstretched):* My darling!

LILLIAN *(Putting her arms around his neck):* My hero!

COUNTESS *(Entering on scene; to audience, with hands raised):* What's a mother to do? *(Curtain)*

THE END

PRODUCTION NOTES

WHEN PIRATES RULED THE SEA

Characters: 3 male; 2 female.

Playing Time: 20 minutes.

Costumes: Captain wears glasses, black pants, white silky shirt, black boots, and has pistol tucked into his belt. Bosun Collins wears ragged, white pants, dirty vest, bandana, chain with medallion, gold, ring-shaped earring, and has dagger in belt. Roger Jolly has on neat white pants, red and white striped shirt, bandana, and carries a handkerchief in pocket. Countess wears 18th-century style dress, lots of jewelry, and is heavily made up. Lillian wears dress in same style and has ribbon in hair.

Properties: Pistols; small vial; two ropes; bundle of clothing; box.

Setting: Captain's private quarters on board *The Scarlet Raven.* Large desk covered with maps, papers, etc., and chair are center. Glove with hook, tankard, eyepatch, glasses, pirate hat, and spyglass are lying on desk. At right stand two crates marked RUM and ALE. Backdrop shows portholes in wooden wall.

Sound: No special effects.

Taking a Bite Out of Crime

Characters

MARGE, *roll call sergeant*
CHIEF HARRIS
MONIKA VON HESS ⎤
EDDY TREDWAY ⎟
ROXIE JOHNSON ⎬ *police officers*
BEN MILLER ⎦
DETECTIVE DRAKE
RICHFIELD
PAMELA HARRIS, *Chief's daughter*
NORA, *housekeeper*

TIME: *The turn of the century.*
SETTING: *Basement squad room of New York City Police Department. The walls are gray. Stairs from upper level curve down into room from up-*

stage left. At stage right is wall in which a sliding panel is concealed. Platform is right; several chairs are left, facing platform.

AT RISE: MONIKA VON HESS, EDDY TREDWAY, ROXIE JOHNSON, *and* BEN MILLER *sit in chairs left.* MARGE *and* CHIEF *are on platform center front;* MARGE *is taking roll call.*

MARGE: Tredway!

EDDY: Here.

MARGE: Johnson!

ROXIE: Present.

MARGE: Miller.

BEN: Here.

MARGE: von Hess!

MONIKA: Here.

MARGE (*Pointing to* MONIKA): I want you all to welcome Detective von Hess, our newest addition from the East Side precinct. She'll be working with us for a few weeks. (*Others ad lib greetings.*)

BEN (*To* MONIKA): Von Hess, eh? Any relation to Professor von Hess?

MONIKA: Yes, he's my father.

BEN (*With a snicker*): Is he still chasing ghosts and ghouls?

MONIKA (*Not amused*): Vampires, to be precise, Lieutenant.

CHIEF: Based on her familiarity with her father's research on the subject, Detective von Hess should be able to shed some light on the criminal who has been stalking our streets.

BEN *(Amused):* No offense, Chief, but what makes her think our crime wave is something she can sink her teeth into?

ROXIE: The attacks on innocent people are hardly a laughing matter, Ben.

CHIEF: Exactly. As I was mentioning to Detective Drake the other evening . . . *(Looks around)* Where is he, by the way?

MARGE *(Checking watch):* He usually comes in right after sunset.

CHIEF: Well, he'll be along, I'm sure. . . . Stopping this wave of killing is top priority. Eddy, let's have the update.

EDDY *(Standing and referring to his notes):* Right, Chief. Dr. Richards has confirmed that each of the victims had a small bite on the side of the neck, the mark of two very sharp fangs. In addition, the victims were completely drained of their blood.

MONIKA: How many victims have there been so far?

EDDY: Twenty-nine.

CHIEF: Actually, Eddy, that figure needs correcting. The thirtieth victim was attacked last Tuesday evening just after sundown. Unlike the others, she has lived to tell of it.

ROXIE *(Anxiously):* Who is she? What did she say?

CHIEF: The latest victim . . . is my daughter, Pamela.

EDDY *(Aghast):* Oh, no! Why didn't someone tell me?

CHIEF: Because of your close relationship with Pamela, I thought it best for you to think she was recovering from the flu.

EDDY *(Frantically):* I have to see her!

MARGE: Take it easy, Eddy.

MONIKA: How did it happen, Chief?

CHIEF: Pamela was returning from her singing lesson and decided to stop by the precinct to see when I'd be home for supper. She said a man jumped out of the shadows and startled her. She fainted and remembers nothing else. Dr. Richards examined her and found two marks on her neck, like those on the other victims.

MONIKA: Where is she now?

CHIEF: Resting at home, under the watchful eye of our housekeeper.

MONIKA: Is anyone else there with them? They shouldn't be alone!

CHIEF: The house is quite secure, Detective von Hess.

MONIKA: I trust you've taken the necessary precautions. Garlic? Wolfsbane?

BEN *(Amused):* You must be joking!

ROXIE: She has a point, Ben. *(To others)* If we really are dealing with a vampire, Pamela is in more danger than we realize.

BEN *(Rising):* All right, all right—if there's cause for alarm, I'll go check on her right now. The house is on my beat. *(To* CHIEF*)* O.K., Chief?

CHIEF: Yes, I guess that's a good idea, Ben—though only a madman would attempt to break into my house.

BEN: Take notes for me, will you, Roxie? *(Exits up stairs)*

EDDY *(Upset):* I think you should have sent me, sir. After all, Pamela and I are nearly engaged.

CHIEF: But you'll be Monika's partner while she's with us, Eddy. I need to have you show her the ropes.

ROXIE: Chief, how long do we have to work the night shift? I mean, people like Ben never complain, but this schedule is driving me crazy.

CHIEF *(Pompously):* Until this bloodthirsty criminal is brought to justice, we're all going to spend our evenings seeking him out.

MONIKA: What about the days? Since a vampire must return each sunrise to the place where he was buried, it might be productive to have a team search for his coffin during the day and destroy it.

EDDY *(Angrily):* I'd rather catch him in person and show him a thing or two! (DRAKE *appears at top of stairs, unnoticed by others.*)

MONIKA: Then I hope you have a good stake handy—the only way to destroy a vampire is to drive a stake through his heart.

DRAKE *(Slowly descending stairs, entering):* The lady seems well versed in vampire superstitions. (RICHFIELD, *zombie-like, follows* DRAKE *down stairs.*)

CHIEF (*Greeting* DRAKE): Well, Drake! I was beginning to wonder where you were.

DRAKE *(Smoothly):* A minor matter detained me, Chief. I took a nap and overslept.

CHIEF (*Pointing to* RICHFIELD): Who's that?

DRAKE: I found him wandering around outside.

MONIKA (*Suspiciously eyeing* RICHFIELD): Perhaps he's another victim of our night prowler.

ROXIE: What's wrong with him? Why doesn't he say anything? (MONIKA *approaches him;* RICHFIELD *stares straight ahead.*)

MONIKA: Hypnosis. *(Waves her hand in front of* RICHFIELD's *eyes)* Vampires have been known to put unsuspecting victims into a trance. The victims lose all memory of who they are.

DRAKE (*Extending his hand gallantly to* MONIKA): I don't believe I've had the pleasure.

MONIKA: Monika von Hess.

DRAKE *(Kissing her hand, then surveying her critically):* von Hess, did you say?

MONIKA: Is my name familiar to you, Detective?

DRAKE *(Abruptly):* No, I don't believe it is.

MONIKA *(Noticing back of* DRAKE's *cape):* Pardon me, but the back of your cape seems—(*She starts to touch it, but he wheels around quickly.*)

DRAKE: You were going to say . . . ?

MONIKA: Your cape seems to be a little dusty . . . almost as if it had been—

DRAKE *(Quickly):* Lying across a dusty path, of course. *(Laughs nervously)* Earlier this evening, as a lady stepped across the street to her carriage, I threw my cape down for her.

ROXIE *(Sighing):* And who said chivalry was dead? *(Scream is heard offstage. All except* RICHFIELD *react.)*

ALL *(Ad lib):* Oh, no! Who was that? What's happened? *(Etc.)*

NORA *(Running down stairs):* Mr. Harris! Mr. Harris! *(Runs to* CHIEF)

CHIEF *(Excitedly):* What is it, Nora? Where is Pamela?

NORA: She is at home, sir.

CHIEF *(Angrily):* I told you not to leave her, even for a minute!

NORA: But the dogs, sir . . . they were howling! I went to close the French doors to Pamela's bedroom when suddenly a huge black bird flew in, right toward her. She screamed and fainted.

CHIEF *(Pushing* NORA *toward stairs):* You should not have left her alone! We must go at once. *(They exit up stairs.)*

EDDY: I'm coming with you! *(Exits)*

ROXIE: Come on, Marge—let's hit the streets. *(They exit up stairs.)*

DRAKE *(With a slight sneer):* Well, Miss von Hess. What do *you* make of all this? You're the expert!

MONIKA *(Coolly):* I think you know the answer as well as I do, Detective Drake. *(Quick curtain)*

*   *   *   *   *

SCENE 2

TIME: *Some time later.*

SETTING: *The same.*

AT RISE: MONIKA *is talking to* BEN. RICHFIELD *stands at right.*

MONIKA: And you didn't see anyone leaving the house?

BEN: Not a soul. *(Shakes his head)* If you ask me, Pamela Harris is pretty high-strung. She probably imagined the whole thing.

MONIKA: You seem well versed in human psychology, Ben.

BEN: After years of experience in this business, you learn to distinguish between what's real and what's imagined. *(Pauses)* Do you know what the Chief is going to do to protect Pamela?

MONIKA: The only thing he can do under the circumstances. He's bringing her here to the station.

BEN: That makes sense. This is the safest place for her to be right now.

MONIKA: I've also asked Eddy to pick up a couple of strands of garlic to pass around.

BEN *(Surprised):* You're really serious about that, aren't you? (DRAKE *appears at top of stairs, unnoticed by* BEN *and* MONIKA.)

MONIKA: I have no doubt that our vampire will search for Pamela here, and when he shows up, he'll be trapped. Garlic stops vampires in their tracks.

DRAKE *(Descending stairs):* Are you quite sure about that, Miss von Hess? I've read that vampires are very clever.

MONIKA: Clever, but not unbeatable.

BEN: You're back soon, Drake. I thought you'd still be out combing the streets. *(To* MONIKA*)* If anyone knows how to track like a bloodhound, it's Drake.

MONIKA *(To* DRAKE*):* I understand, Detective Drake, that you have an impressive record in the department.

DRAKE *(Smiling):* I daresay that's an exaggeration. *(Crosses to* RICHFIELD, *looks him over)* He hasn't moved, I see. *(Waves his hand in front of* RICHFIELD's *face)*

BEN: Perhaps he's waiting for directions from his master. *(With her back to* DRAKE, MONIKA *takes a small compact from her pocket, opens it and looks into it.)* Monika tells me that someone in a trance will take certain actions, but won't know why. Fascinating, isn't it? (MONIKA, *still looking into compact mirror, frowns and shakes her head.)*

DRAKE *(To* BEN*):* I suppose so, if you believe all that. (MONIKA *puts compact back into pocket.)*

BEN: I guess you've heard that the Chief is bringing his daughter Pamela here for protection. Monika's going to distribute garlic to everyone in the station.

DRAKE: Really. Well, it's good to take precautions.

BEN *(Checking his pocketwatch):* I'd better be on

my way. It's almost sunrise, and our quarry may be skulking around familiar haunts, looking for a bite.

MONIKA: Where are you going, Ben?

BEN: To the Blood Bank. It's on my beat. *(Starts to exit.* DRAKE *blocks his path.)*

DRAKE: Actually, Ben, I was planning to check out the Blood Bank myself. Why don't you stay here and keep Miss von Hess company? *(Exits quickly up stairs)*

MONIKA: He's certainly a strange one.

BEN: Yes, and hard to get to know. *(Pause)* Come to think of it, I don't even know where he lives.

MONIKA: Is there a personnel file on him? I'd like to take a look at it.

BEN: I'm sure there is. Ask Sergeant White upstairs. He keeps the files. (MONIKA *exits.* BEN *starts to follow, then pauses in front of* RICHFIELD. *He looks around, then speaks to* RICHFIELD.) When I snap my fingers, I want you to close your eyes. *(Snaps fingers;* RICHFIELD's *eyes close, and* BEN *smiles.)* Very good. Now, take a nice nap. I'll have work for you later. *(Exits up stairs. Curtain)*

* * * * *

SCENE 3

TIME: *An hour later.*

SETTING: *The same.*

AT RISE: EDDY *comes downstairs, then turns to*

help PAMELA *down. She wears a hooded cape over her dress and appears quite frightened.*

EDDY *(Kindly):* It's all right, Pamela. As long as you're with me, you're perfectly safe. (MONIKA, *reading a file, comes down the stairs, turns toward* EDDY *and* PAMELA.) Just sit down and rest.

PAMELA *(Sitting):* Oh, Eddy, it was so horrible! I'm still shaky.

MONIKA *(To* EDDY): Eddy, did you bring the garlic?

EDDY: Yes. *(Takes two garlic bulbs from pocket, hands one to* MONIKA) One bulb for you, and one for me.

MONIKA: What about one for Pamela?

EDDY: With the two of us here to protect her, I didn't think she needed any garlic.

PAMELA: I'm so frightened. I hope it's safe here.

MONIKA *(Shaking her head):* I don't think we should take any chances. *(Looks through file again)*

EDDY: What's so interesting in that file?

MONIKA: Well, for one thing—(PAMELA *sneezes.*)

EDDY: Oh, no. I think she's catching a cold. Monika, would you mind running up and getting us some coffee?

MONIKA: Not at all. Just don't let Pamela out of your sight. *(Exits up stairs)*

PAMELA: It's so sweet of you to look after me this way, Eddy.

EDDY: Pamela *(Sits next to her),* surely you've noticed how crazy I am about you. As a matter of fact—when all of this is over—I'm planning to ask your father for your hand in marriage.

PAMELA *(In surprise):* Eddy! Do you really mean it? *(Matter-of-factly)* Can you afford it?

EDDY *(Dramatically):* We'll be rich enough in love. And besides, my uncle can always use an extra clerk at his store.

PAMELA: Won't you get tired working all day here and then going to your uncle's store?

EDDY: Actually, dearest, I thought perhaps such a job would suit you.

PAMELA *(Distressed):* Are you saying that you want me to work? Every day? In a *store*?

EDDY *(Quickly):* Only part-time, till we can save some money. And we'll find a charming flat on West 23rd.

PAMELA *(Disappointed):* Not in Branfair Heights?

EDDY: Branfair Heights, my sweet, is a little rich for my blood! *(Sound of wind howling is heard, and lights flicker.)*

PAMELA *(Jumping up):* What was that noise?

EDDY: Just the wind, Pamela. Don't worry. We're perfectly safe. *(Lights go out, and* PAMELA *screams.)* Pamela! Pamela! Where are you? Wait—let me find a match. . . . I know I have one here somewhere. . . . Ah, here we are. *(He lights match and "relights" a lamp.* PAMELA *is lying on floor, her back to audience.* EDDY *rushes to her side.)* Pamela! Oh, no, she's fainted. *(Calling loudly up stairs)* Monika! Come quickly! Pamela's fainted! *(As he calls out, the panel in wall slowly slides back; mist swirls out of opening, and* BEN *steps out.* EDDY *doesn't notice him.)* It can't take that long to get coffee. I hope Monika's all right. (*Turns and sees* BEN) Ben! How did you get down here? I thought Pamela and I were alone.

BEN (*Menacingly*): On the contrary, Eddy. I've been waiting for you.

EDDY: Well, you should have said something. You gave me a real scare.

BEN (*Looking down at* PAMELA): I see you've brought Pamela to me.

EDDY: Yes. The Chief thought it would be best . . . (*Puzzled*) What do you mean, I brought her to *you*?

BEN (*Coldly*): Pamela is to be my bride for all eternity.

EDDY (*Approaching* BEN): Listen, Ben, I know you're a smooth talker and all the ladies fall for you, but not Pamela. She's already spoken for.

BEN: I beg to differ with you.

EDDY (*Calling up stairs*): Monika! What are you doing up there? What's taking so long?

BEN (*Pleasantly*): Oh, she can't hear you, Eddy. A sleeping potion in the coffee has taken care of that.

EDDY (*Belligerently*): Are you playing games with me?

BEN (*Shaking his head*): You really haven't figured it out yet, have you?

EDDY (*Confused*): Figured *what* out?

BEN: The identity of the mysterious night stalker. Surely I've given you enough clues.

EDDY: You mean that all the attacks are between sunset and sunrise, and they're all in the vicinity of the precinct house, and *(Suddenly stops in realization)* . . .

BEN *(Smugly):* Go on.

EDDY *(Horrified):* It's you! You're the night stalker!

BEN: And now that you know . . . *(Approaches* EDDY*)* you'll have to pay the price.

EDDY: Not yet! *(Pulls garlic from pocket.* BEN *turns away.)* You're trapped now. The only way out *(Backs toward* RICHFIELD*)* is up those stairs. And you can't get there from here, not as long as I have this garlic.

BEN: You haven't beaten me yet.

EDDY: Haven't I? Stick around until sunrise and watch!

BEN: I think you've forgotten someone. *(Calls)* Richfield! (RICHFIELD *opens his eyes, turns head toward* BEN.*)*

EDDY: Who's Richfield?

BEN: You'll see. *(To* RICHFIELD*)* Take care of him, will you? (RICHFIELD *hits* EDDY *over head;* EDDY *falls to ground.)* Excellent, Richfield.

RICHFIELD *(In monotone):* What do you wish me to do next, master?

BEN: You must build a fire, Richfield. A very big fire that will consume this entire building. And while you're busy doing that, I shall take Pamela to my underground vault. It's my good fortune that the secret room is fireproof. *(Chuckles, to* RICHFIELD*)*

Go, Richfield. The others will be back soon.

RICHFIELD (*In monotone*): Yes, master. (*Exits up stairs*)

BEN (*Crossing to stand over* PAMELA): For three hundred years, I have searched for the perfect love. And now, my dearest Pamela, you will be mine, mine forever! (*Turns her over. The hood falls back to reveal* MONIKA, *who holds garlic bulb to* BEN's *face*)

MONIKA: That's a date you won't be able to keep!

BEN (*Turning away from her*): Monika!

MONIKA (*As* EDDY *starts to stir*): Eddy! Wake up! (EDDY *scrambles to his feet, retrieves his garlic and holds it up to* BEN's *face*.) I'm afraid, Ben, that your infamous nights are over. The sun will be up soon . . . and then there's no escape for you.

BEN (*Laughing evilly*): That's where you're mistaken, dear lady. (*Snaps fingers, lights go out*)

EDDY: Where is he? I can't see a thing!

MONIKA: Stay by the steps, Eddy. I'll find a light. (*After a moment, lights come up.* BEN *has disappeared.*)

EDDY: He's gone! But that's impossible! There's no way he could have left the room.

CHIEF (*Calling down stairs*); He left all right, Eddy, but he didn't get far. (*Comes down stairs, pushing* DRAKE *ahead of him*)

DRAKE: See here, Chief! You're making a big mistake!

CHIEF: Here's your vampire, Monika! *(In disgust)* A member of my own precinct, too!

MONIKA *(Shaking her head):* No, Chief—you have it all wrong. Drake's not your vampire.

CHIEF *(Blustering):* But certainly there were enough clues!

MONIKA: Those clues were planted to throw us off the track of the real vampire. In our quest for justice, we nearly made a grave mistake.

CHIEF: But when you offered to trade places with my daughter—

MONIKA: It was to trap the real villain. When I glanced in my mirror earlier, I noticed that Drake was reflected in it, but Ben was not. And when I read the personnel files, I had further proof of Drake's innocence.

CHIEF *(Shocked):* So Ben is the night stalker! I can't believe it!

ROXIE *(Pushing RICHFIELD down stairs):* O.K., move along. *(To CHIEF)* I caught this character playing with matches, Chief. I think he planned to burn the station down.

CHIEF *(Sternly; to RICHFIELD):* What do you have to say for yourself? *(RICHFIELD stares straight ahead, as if in trance.)*

MONIKA *(Checking her watch):* Sunrise is just a few minutes off. *(Paces around room)* The vampire's coffin can't be very far from here. *(Suddenly)* Wait a minute! He mentioned an underground

vault that's fireproof. That means it must be somewhere underneath the station house!

EDDY: Good guess, Monika!

MONIKA *(Crossing to wall):* There must be a secret
panel around here someplace. *(Taps on walls)*

PAMELA *(Running down stairs to* EDDY): Oh,
Eddy! Is it over yet?

EDDY: Almost, Pamela. (MONIKA *continues to tap
wall, then slides panel back.)*

MONIKA: Aha! There's only one way to handle a
vampire. I kept a tool box here in the corner.
*(Goes to side of stage, pulls stake and hammer
out of tool box)*

EDDY: This could be dangerous, Monika. Do you
need help?

MONIKA *(Shaking head):* No. I can handle it. *(Exits
through opening in wall)*

EDDY *(Admiringly):* Now, there's a woman after
my heart! *(After a moment, an agonizing yell is
heard.* PAMELA *screams and faints.* DRAKE *and*
RICHFIELD *both yell and hold their heads as if in
pain.* EDDY *runs toward opening.)* Monika! Are
you O.K.? *(There is no answer.)*

RICHFIELD *(Looking down at his pajamas in disgust; speaking normally):* Good heavens! What
am I doing in these tacky clothes?

DRAKE *(Looking around in puzzlement):* And what
am I doing in this tacky basement?

CHIEF *(Puzzled):* I beg your pardon?

RICHFIELD: What's going on here? Where am I? *(Suddenly)* I've got it. It's a joke, right? And you're all in on it?

DRAKE *(To* RICHFIELD): Excuse me, but what play are we doing? I seem to have a lapse of memory.

RICHFIELD: Play? What are you talking about?

DRAKE *(Scratching his head):* If memory serves, I had just stepped outside between scenes for a breath of fresh air, and . . . I don't remember what happened next.

RICHFIELD: That sounds like what happened to me. Except that I stepped outside to let out the cat, and—*(Makes chopping motion)* zap!

CHIEF *(Bewildered):* When did all this happen?

RICHFIELD: Oh, it couldn't have been more than a couple of hours ago.

MONIKA *(Re-entering):* I'm afraid it's been longer than that, Mr. Richfield.

EDDY *(Relieved):* Monika! You're all right!

RICHFIELD: How long, then?

MONIKA: You've been missing for five years.

RICHFIELD *(Stunned): Five years!*

MONIKA *(Nodding):* You simply disappeared one night and were never seen again. I thought you looked vaguely familiar when I first saw you. *(To* CHIEF) The East Side was handling the case, and we were all completely baffled. We never suspected that Richfield was in a trance.

EDDY *(Pointing to* DRAKE): So who's he?

MONIKA: That's Drake Carrington, distinguished actor of the London stage. Like Mr. Richfield here, he fell under the vampire's spell.

DRAKE *(Outraged):* Why, the scoundrel!

RICHFIELD *(In disbelief):* I can't believe I've been out of circulation all this time. My parents must have given me up for dead. Would you mind giving them a call to explain? They're in the book—the Atlantic Richfields. (PAMELA *starts to stir.* RICHFIELD *looks at her.)* Say—what's wrong with her?

CHIEF: That's my daughter, Pamela. She faints rather easily.

PAMELA (*Opening her eyes and seeing* RICHFIELD): Oh, hello. I'm Pamela Harris.

RICHFIELD *(Surprised):* Pamela Harris! Is it really? *(Enthusiastically; helping her to her feet)* Malcolm Richfield. Do you remember me?

PAMELA *(Surprised):* Why, Malcolm! *(Recovering quickly)* Yes, of course, I do! We played croquet at the Wallaces. Let me see, it was springtime, six years ago, wasn't it?

RICHFIELD: Yes, that's right. My family lives in the Heights now. Branfair Heights. At least that's where I think we live.

PAMELA *(Coyly):* How charming. (*To* CHIEF) Father, do you mind if Malcolm walks me home now?

CHIEF: Yes, I suppose it's all right. I'll see you at home later.

EDDY *(In dismay):* But, Pamela! What about me?

PAMELA *(Approaching* EDDY; *apologetically):* I'm sorry, Eddy. It was fun while it lasted. *(Exits up stairs with* RICHFIELD. EDDY *looks disconsolate.)*

ROXIE *(Approaching* DRAKE): Have I ever told you how much I adore the theater?

DRAKE: Do you really? *(Offers her his arm as they go up stairs)* Did you ever see me perform *Hamlet*? As I recall, I was quite good. I also played Dracula once, magnificently. *(They exit.)*

CHIEF: Let's close the book on this one, shall we, Tredway?

EDDY: I'll write up the report right away, Chief. (CHIEF *exits.* EDDY *sits, with head in hands.)*

MONIKA: What's the matter, Eddy?

EDDY *(Miserably):* Pamela didn't even say goodbye.

MONIKA: Well, if you want an honest opinion, she didn't really seem your type.

EDDY: She had good bloodlines, though.

MONIKA: Even if you were at cross purposes?

EDDY: I suppose you're right. Sometimes she was a real pain in the neck. And all that fainting!

MONIKA: How would you like to continue this conversation over breakfast? I'm famished!

EDDY *(Smiling):* I'd love to. *(They exit up stairs. Curtain)*

THE END

PRODUCTION NOTES

TAKING A BITE OUT OF CRIME

Characters: 5 male; 5 female.

Playing Time: 25 minutes.

Costumes: Marge and Chief wear police uniforms of the period. Other police officers are in "undercover" garb; Monika and Eddy wear similar outfits—knickers, sweaters, and caps; Roxie wears bulky clothes, old boots, and gloves without fingers; Ben is outfitted as a city gentleman—suit and hat; Detective Drake wears evening outfit with black cape lined in red satin; Pamela wears hooded cape over dress of the period; Richfield wears pajamas; Nora wears maid's uniform.

Properties: Several sheets of paper for Eddy; small compact with mirror; pocketwatch; several bulbs of garlic; file folder; matches; tool box containing stake and hammer.

Setting: Basement squad room of New York City Police Department. Walls are gray. Stairs from upper level curve down into room from upstage left. At stage right is wall in which a sliding panel is concealed. Platform is right; several chairs are left, facing platform.

Lighting: Flickering and blackouts, as indicated.

Sound: Wind howling.

Special Effects: Dry ice creates mist when panel wall slides back in Scene 3.

The Silver-Tongued Slicker of Sassafras Flat

Characters

MARABELLE MURPHY, *owner of the Sassafras Cafe*
FRANK FEENEY, *owner of the general store*
JOSHUA JONES, *a visitor from the Big City*
MAISIE MUGREW, *the mayor's sister*
LINNIE MAE GRUMPLEMEYER, *a disgruntled matron*
ELLY MULDOON, *a lady in distress*

TIME: *Summer, 1900.*
SETTING: *The Sassafras Cafe, in Sassafras Flat. There are several tables and chairs. Upstage window looks out onto quiet street. Newspaper is lying on counter, up right. Plates, cups, pies, and kettle are on counter. Entrance, working door, is left.*

AT RISE: FRANK *and* JOSHUA *are seated at table, polishing off the remains of dinner.* MARABELLE *steps out from behind counter, and crosses to table.*

MARABELLE *(Wiping hands on apron):* How are you boys doin'?

FRANK *(Leaning back; contentedly):* I'm stuffed fuller than a Thanksgiving turkey!

JOSHUA *(Pointing to his empty plate):* Ma'am, that was one meal fit for a king!

MARABELLE *(Coaxingly; to* FRANK): Are you sure I can't talk you into another slice of rhubarb pie?

FRANK: It was really good, Marabelle.

JOSHUA *(Teasingly):* One more bite, Frank, and I'm gonna have to roll you home like a pickle barrel!

FRANK *(Shaking his head):* Guess we'd better settle up. *(To* MARABELLE) How much do I owe you, Marabelle?

MARABELLE *(Looking at* JOSHUA's *empty plate):* Let me see—you had the chicken fricasse, potatoes, buttered beets, a cup of coffee and green apple pie. *(Pause)* That'll be 35 cents. (JOSHUA *whistles.)*

FRANK *(Anxiously):* How 'bout my tab?

MARABELLE: Hm-m-m . . . roast beef, mashed potatoes, rhubarb pie and buttermilk? Thirty cents even.

FRANK *(Aghast):* Highway robbery! *(He and* JOSHUA *fumble for change.)*

MARABELLE: Goin' to get higher, come winter.

Prices keep goin' up. (*Hands on hips; defiantly*) Can't get a pound of chicken for less than seven cents any more . . . (*Shakes head*) and a pound of beef's gone up to ten.

FRANK: Can't get much higher.

JOSHUA: Already higher in New York.

FRANK: How high?

JOSHUA: At one of those fancy society restaurants, you know what you'd pay for a fine meal like this?

MARABELLE: Give us a clue.

JOSHUA: Better than that—I'll give you the answer. (MARABELLE *and* FRANK *bend forward eagerly*.) Ninety-seven cents.

FRANK: What's the world coming to?

MARABELLE (*Sitting down next to* JOSHUA): Have you really been to the big city, Mr. Jones?

JOSHUA (*Covering her hand with his*): Just call me Joshua.

MARABELLE: Have you really been to New York City, Joshua?

FRANK: Why, Joshua's been halfway round the world and back again, haven't you, Joshua?

JOSHUA: Oh, now, Frank, don't you get me braggin'. This little lady here would be bored silly. . . .

MARABELLE: Is New York City as pretty as they say it is?

JOSHUA (*Winking at her*): Once you get me talking, Marabelle, you may have to part with another cup of that fine coffee.

MARABELLE (*Reaching for his cup*): I'll get it.

JOSHUA *(Taking cup from table):* Wouldn't think of it. You just rest here a minute and I'll get it. *(Crosses to counter, holding cup)*

MARABELLE *(To* FRANK): Now, there's what I call a gentleman, Frank. All that travel and those fancy duds. He must make a heap of money. What'd you say he does?

FRANK: Joshua is what they call an entrepreneur.

MARABELLE *(Nodding; knowledgeably):* Foreigner, huh?

FRANK: No, an entrepreneur is—*(Door bursts open, and* MAISIE MUGREW, *very agitated, runs in.)*

MAISIE: Robbed! I've been robbed! (JOSHUA *ducks behind counter.* MARABELLE *rises and runs to* MAISIE.)

MARABELLE: Why, Maisie Mugrew, what on earth are you talking about? *(Puts arm around* MAISIE's *shoulder)*

MAISIE *(Very agitated):* Right in broad daylight! And right under my very nose!

FRANK *(Crossing to* MAISIE): Calm yourself, Miss Maisie, and tell us what happened.

MAISIE: He seemed like such a nice young man.

FRANK *and* MARABELLE: Who?

MAISIE *(Continuing):* He said he knew my dear departed Charlie, and the next thing I knew, I'd been robbed!

MARABELLE: What did he take?

MAISIE *(Pulling large gold locket out of her pocket):* This!

FRANK *(Scratching his head):* If he stole the locket, how come you still have it?

MAISIE: He took my five dollars and said it was the last payment for this piece of fine jewelry.

FRANK *(Examining locket):* It seems fine enough to me. Why are you so riled?

MAISIE: He said my late departed Charlie was buying it before he met his untimely demise.

FRANK: That was nice of Charlie.

MAISIE *(Impatiently):* Charlie never bought me a present in his life! But that fast-talking salesman didn't know that. He was just taking advantage of my bereavement!

MARABELLE: A salesman, you say?

MAISIE: I've never seen him around these parts before. Tall, good-looking, little mustache . . .

FRANK: Hm-m-m . . . that could be most anybody. Maybe Joshua's seen him. *(Turns)* Hey, Joshua! Where are you? *(Puzzled)* That's funny, he was just here a minute ago.

MAISIE: Well, I've got to find the sheriff and tell my brother the mayor there's trouble brewing right here in Sassafras Flat.

MARABELLE *(As MAISIE exits):* We'll keep an eye out for him.

FRANK: Imagine that! Right here in Sassafras Flat!

MARABELLE: Where'd your friend Mr. Jones go, Frank?

JOSHUA *(Standing and holding the top of his head):* Got one mighty hard counter back here, ma'am.

MARABELLE: Why, Mr. Jones! *(Running to him)*

Are you all right? What on earth happened?

JOSHUA: I'm not sure, ma'am. The last thing I recall, I spilled a little of this fine coffee and bent down to clean it up. Next thing I knew, I was seeing stars!

FRANK: You missed a lot of excitement, Joshua.

JOSHUA: Really?

MARABELLE: It seems there's a con artist running loose in Sassafras Flat.

JOSHUA (*Rubbing head*): You don't say.

FRANK: You feeling all right, Joshua?

JOSHUA: I think I'll sit a spell, Frank. Could I take a look at the newspaper?

MARABELLE: I have it right over here, Mr. Jones. (*Gets it for him*)

JOSHUA: Much obliged, ma'am.

FRANK: Now, what were we talking about before all this excitement?

MARABELLE: New York City!

FRANK: And how they charge 97 cents for dinner.

MARABELLE: Oh, Frank, your mind's always on food.

FRANK: Just think. If they're charging 97 cents for dinner now, in another 50 years, it'll probably be up to two whole dollars!

MARABELLE (*Shaking her head*): Folks are going to starve right outside a cafe door just because they can't afford to walk in!

FRANK: If that's what they call progress, I hope it passes us by!

MARABELLE (*To* JOSHUA): Is it true that everyone in New York City has a motor car, Mr. Jones?

JOSHUA: It's sad but true, Miss Marabelle. Folks say it'll spread west like wildfire—everybody will be driving every which way. (LINNIE MAE GRUMPLEMEYER *rushes in.*)

LINNIE: Help! Help!

MARABELLE *(Taken aback):* Why Linnie Mae Grumplemeyer! What on earth is the matter?

FRANK *(To* JOSHUA): That's Linnie Mae Grumplemeyer, Joshua. She complains about everything. (JOSHUA *glances at her, then holds newspaper in front of his face.*)

LINNIE: As sure as I live and breathe, Marabelle Murphy, it's a scandal!

MARABELLE: Scandal? In Sassafras Flat? What do you mean?

LINNIE: Last evening a gentleman came to call on me!

MARABELLE: That's the scandal?

FRANK *(Smirking):* Sounds more like a miracle to me.

MARABELLE: What did he want?

LINNIE: He wanted five dollars . . . *(Holding up gold locket)* for this!

FRANK: That looks familiar.

MARABELLE *(Examining it):* Why, it's engraved . . . and from your dear departed Octavius!

LINNIE *(Taking locket):* And that's exactly what's wrong!

FRANK: What's wrong?

LINNIE: He never went by Octavius in his life. It was his given name, but folks around here called him Jack. You don't suppose on the verge of his demise he'd go back to Octavius!

MARABELLE: Guess not. Did you ask the man who sold you the locket?

LINNIE: No, I was so upset that I didn't even open the package until this morning. When I saw the inscription, I just knew something was wrong.

FRANK: Sounds like the same fellow who robbed Maisie Mugrew.

MARABELLE (*To* LINNIE): What did he look like?

LINNIE: Good looking, tall, little mustache. All sweet talk.

FRANK (*To* JOSHUA): Have you seen anyone like that around here, Joshua?

JOSHUA (*Keeping paper in front of his face):* No.

MARABELLE (*To* LINNIE): Have you notified the authorities?

LINNIE: I've done better than that. An authority is on his way to town—even as we speak. He'll clear this up. Mark my words! (*Exits*)

MARABELLE: What a vile cad—to take advantage of Miss Maisie and Linnie Mae!

FRANK: What do you think, Joshua?

JOSHUA (*Folding paper):* Shameful, downright shameful. They ought to lock that fellow up and throw away the key! (*Takes out pocketwatch and looks at it*)

FRANK (*Noticing):* Joshua, how come you keep lookin' at your daddy's pocketwatch?

JOSHUA: Have to catch a train, Frank.

FRANK: You're leaving Sassafras Flat? I thought you'd taken a liking to this place. I was even hopin' you'd be my partner.

JOSHUA: Do you mean you could get me a job in this town?

FRANK: Sure! You could get yourself a fine little store like mine, and spend your days stocking the shelves and flirtin' with the ladies.

JOSHUA: There's not much money in a store, is there?

FRANK *(Folding arms in satisfaction):* I got myself a raise last month—21 cents an hour!

MARABELLE: I hate to impose on you boys, but would one of you mind watching the cafe for a short spell? *(Taking letter out of apron)* I've got to get over to the telegraph office before it closes.

FRANK: Gosh, Miss Marabelle, I have to get back to my store and—

JOSHUA *(With a gallant bow):* Allow me!

MARABELLE *(To* FRANK): Now, here's a real gentleman! *(Exits)*

FRANK *(Exiting):* See you later, Joshua!

JOSHUA *(Glancing out door for a few moments, then picking up newspaper):* Let me see, where are they? *(Reading)* Ah—"William Barnsworth, husband of Sara" . . . very good . . . "Davenport, Bernard"—no, that won't do. "A confirmed bachelor." Hm-m-m—"Rivers, Edward J.; Wife, Elizabeth Anne." *(Puts paper down and acts out a meeting with woman)* "My dear Elizabeth Anne.

(Pretends to kiss her hand) May I say how thoroughly devastated I was to hear about poor Edward, I truly was. Why, just a week ago, Edward asked that I deliver this personally. *(Holding up gold locket)* He said it was to commemorate the anniversary of the first day he ever laid eyes on you!" *(Sighs, wipes a tear away, then puts watch back into pocket)* Oh, Joshua, you're getting too good at this, you silver-tongued master of deception! *(Addressing audience)* Oh, I know what you're thinking—that it's not an honorable way to make a living. True, true. But is there really harm in telling them sentimental stories they long to hear? *(Laughs)* And while their hearts fill with love, my pockets fill with riches! (ELLY MULDOON, *sobbing into handkerchief, enters.* JOSHUA *approaches her.)* Pardon me, ma'am, but is that a tear in your eye?

ELLY *(Sniffing):* One of several, as a matter of fact. *(Looks around)* Have you seen Marabelle Murphy?

JOSHUA: She stepped out for just a moment, ma'am. Is there anything I might do to assist you? Miss . . .

ELLY: Muldoon. Elly Muldoon. *(Extends hand)*

JOSHUA *(Taking her hand):* Joshua Jones at your service, ma'am. Just say the word and I'll swim an ocean, scale a mountain . . .

ELLY: Would you pour me a cup of coffee?

JOSHUA: Whatever you say. Why don't you just sit a spell and tell me what's wrong.

ELLY *(Sitting at table):* I'm pleased by your attention, sir . . . but I'm afraid I don't understand it, you bein' a stranger and all.

JOSHUA *(Bringing her cup):* Why, strangers are just friends you haven't met yet, Miss Muldoon.

ELLY: It's Mrs. Muldoon.

JOSHUA: Oh. Well then, your husband's one lucky man, Mrs. Muldoon—lucky man, indeed. *(She starts crying again.)* Have I said something wrong, ma'am?

ELLY: It's about my husband, Mr. Jones. You see, he's late.

JOSHUA: Don't worry your head about it, ma'am, I've been late a time or two myself.

ELLY: But you don't understand.

JOSHUA: 'Course I do, ma'am. It's nothing to worry your pretty head about.

ELLY: What I mean, Mr. Jones, is that George got himself run over by a motorcar.

JOSHUA *(Appearing shocked; with sympathy):* My condolences, ma'am. *(Pauses)* So he's . . . gone?

ELLY: Yes. And just three weeks short of our first anniversary. (JOSHUA *stands and paces a moment.)*

JOSHUA *(Shaking his head):* It couldn't be—no, it couldn't be . . .

ELLY: Couldn't be what, Mr. Jones?

JOSHUA: Nothing, ma'am. Nothing at all.

ELLY: Please tell me what put that furrow in your brow?

JOSHUA *(Slowly):* You say his name was George Muldoon?

ELLY: Yes.

JOSHUA: What was his middle name?

ELLY: Henry. (JOSHUA *shakes his head in dismay.)* Is something wrong?

JOSHUA *(Crossing to table and taking her hands):* It pains me to speak about it. . . .

ELLY: Speak about what?

JOSHUA *(Sighing heavily):* I saw your husband just a few weeks back.

ELLY *(In surprise):* No!

JOSHUA: Oh, yes. Matter of fact, that's what I'm doing here in Sassafras Flat. I made the trip just to see him.

ELLY: What ever for, Mr. Jones? I don't recall him mentioning your name.

JOSHUA: He invited me to supper, too. Though, of course, now—

ELLY: Don't be silly, Mr. Jones. If George invited you—

JOSHUA: No, ma'am, I wouldn't impose on you in your bereavement. *(Rising)* I'll just be on my way. *(Starts to exit)*

ELLY *(Adamantly):* Please don't go! I insist!

JOSHUA *(Turning):* I can't refuse a request like that, now can I, ma'am?

ELLY: So you had business of some sort with George?

JOSHUA: That I did, though I don't suppose I ought to speak about it now, seein' as how George Henry's no longer with us.

ELLY: Do tell me, Mr. Jones. (JOSHUA *scratches chin*) Please?

JOSHUA: He was buyin' you a present.

ELLY: It must have been for our anniversary.

JOSHUA *(Snapping fingers):* His very words, Mrs. Muldoon.

ELLY: George was always planning little surprises.

JOSHUA: Anyway, this bein' a special occasion and all, I was lettin' George buy your present on credit. One more payment, and it would be his, free and clear. *(Frowning)* He was going to pay me when I got to town.

ELLY: Oh, dear! What was the present?

JOSHUA: I really shouldn't show you, ma'am, seein' how I have to take it back to New York.

ELLY: Please? Just a glance?

JOSHUA *(Slowly withdrawing locket from his pocket and handing it to her):* George picked it out himself. He was even going to have it inscribed.

ELLY: What would it have said?

JOSHUA: Now, you mustn't torment yourself.

ELLY: Still, I'd like to know.

JOSHUA *(With hand over heart):* To the one who stole my heart!

ELLY: Oh, my! *(At that moment, MAISIE and LIN-*

NIE MAE *enter.)*

MAISIE: It sounds like the same one! (JOSHUA *quickly leans forward to kiss* ELLY, *and thus, hide his face.)*

LINNIE: It has to be, I'm sure of it!

MAISIE *(Looking around):* Where's Marabelle?

LINNIE: Well, she's not here now.

MAISIE: Nobody here . . . except a couple of love bugs. Let's go. *(They exit.)*

JOSHUA *(Pulling away):* Forgive me, ma'am, but I momentarily forgot myself.

ELLY: Both of us did, I think. *(Admiring locket)* It's really beautiful. (JOSHUA *reaches for locket.)* How much did George owe you . . . for the last payment?

JOSHUA *(Hesitating):* Guess there's no harm in tellin' you. *(Clears his throat)* Seven dollars even.

ELLY *(Reluctantly):* I'm afraid I don't have that kind of money. *(Hands it back)*

JOSHUA *(Shaking his head):* That's a shame. *(Putting it into his pocket)*

ELLY: May I see the locket just one more time? *(He pulls it out and hands it to her again.)* It's like the kind you see in the wish book.

JOSHUA *(Scratching chin):* I could let you have it for six dollars.

ELLY: It's nice of you, Mr. Jones, but times being what they are . . .

JOSHUA: You know, I think ol' George would be mighty disappointed if I couldn't make a special exception. Tell you what I'll do. I'll let you have it for five, and I'll make up the difference out of my own pocket. *(Presses it into her hand)* You can get it inscribed later yourself.

ELLY *(Exuberantly):* Mr. Jones—you are just about the finest gentleman I have ever known! *(Rummages in purse for money)*

JOSHUA: Is that a fact?

ELLY: Next to my daddy, of course. Why, you'll just have to meet him sometime.

JOSHUA: Why, I'd be delighted to meet your daddy! What does he do?

ELLY *(Proudly):* He's a federal marshal.

JOSHUA *(Coughing, nervously):* Admirable profession, ma'am. *(Looks at pocketwatch)* I don't mean to rush you, but I have a train to catch.

ELLY: Are you leaving town already, Mr. Jones?

JOSHUA: Don't want to overstay my welcome.

ELLY: And here I was hoping you'd get a chance to meet my daddy—I'm expecting him for supper.

JOSHUA: I'll just have to take myself a raincheck on that, ma'am. *(Holds out hand for money)*

ELLY: Sorry to detain you, Mr. Jones. It's just that there's something I thought you'd like to know about . . .

JOSHUA: What's that?

ELLY *(Quickly snapping handcuff on his wrist and the other on hers):* I'm following in my daddy's footsteps.

JOSHUA *(In alarm):* What! (MARABELLE *and* FRANK *enter.*)

MARABELLE *(Excitedly):* You mean to say they

looked familiar because they all came from your store, Frank?

FRANK: I can't understand it, Marabelle. I thought maybe the inventory was wrong, but I counted them over again, and there are three definitely missing.

MARABELLE (*Noticing* ELLY): Why, Elly Muldoon! When did you get to town?

ELLY: Just arrived, Marabelle. Miss Maisie and Linnie Mae told me you'd want to know.

MARABELLE (*Seeing handcuffs*): I see you got yourself a man, Elly.

FRANK: Why, it's Joshua!

ELLY: He's also the Silver-Tongued Slicker of Sassafras Flat.

FRANK: The one they're sendin' a federal marshal to arrest?

ELLY: One and the same. Only Daddy's rounding up some rustlers, so he made me a deputy and sent me on ahead.

MARABELLE (*To* FRANK): Elly's been goin' to detective school.

JOSHUA (*To* ELLY): It's a powerful shame, ma'am. (*Indicating locket*) That fine jewelry would have done you justice!

ELLY: Not as fine a justice as this (*Indicating handcuffs*) fancy bracelet's going to do you!

JOSHUA (*To* FRANK): You have to help me, Frank! I'm in a jam!

MARABELLE: You'd better believe it, Mr. Jones—your goose is cooked! Yes, Joshua, you're finally going to get your just desserts!

FRANK: Gosh—all this talk about food, I could eat a horse!

MARABELLE: Sorry, Frank, we're fresh out!

FRANK: Then I'll have to settle for just desserts—like apple pie and rhubarb pie and peach pie and—

MARABELLE *(Laughing as she crosses room):* Follow me!

FRANK *(Indicating* MARABELLE; *smiling):* Woman after my heart!

MARABELLE *(Indicating* FRANK): Man after my cooking.

JOSHUA *(Sighing):* And numbers . . . after my name. *(Curtain)*

THE END

PRODUCTION NOTES

THE SILVER-TONGUED SLICKER OF SASSAFRAS FLAT

Characters: 4 female; 2 male.

Playing Time: 20 minutes.

Costumes: Turn-of-the-century clothing. Joshua wears mustache, coat, and has gold locket and pocketwatch in pocket. Marabelle has on apron, with letter in pocket. Elly carries purse, which holds gun and handcuffs.

Properties: Three gold lockets; coins.

Setting: Sassafras Cafe, with several tables with checked tablecloths, and chairs. Upstage window looks out onto quiet street. Newspaper is lying on counter, which is up right. Plates, cups, pies, and kettle are on counter. Entrance, working door, is left.

Sound and Lighting: No special effects.

Ghostwriter or Ghost?

Characters

ROGER BRIDESMITH, *a famous novelist*
BERNIE DRAKE, *talented but obscure ghostwriter*
CYNTHIA CRUTSINGER, *Roger's fiancée*

TIME: *The present, a spring afternoon.*
SETTING: *Parlor of Crumbling Gables, a mansion on the Eastern seaboard. A desk, cluttered with typewriter, books, pencils, files, stands center, and bookcase full of books is right. Entrance is left. Artifacts from old sailing ships round out the decor. Curtains are down right.*
AT RISE: ROGER BRIDESMITH *enters. He is well-dressed, and is in the process of tying his tie.* BERNIE DRAKE, *who wears jeans, sneakers, a sweater, and glasses, follows.*
BERNIE *(In protest):* You'll never get away with it, Roger.

ROGER *(Laughing):* Nonsense! She's crazy about me.

BERNIE *(Impatiently):* How crazy do you think she'll be about you when she finds out you can't even write two lines on a postcard?

ROGER: That's the point—she won't find out at all.

BERNIE: You don't think she'll catch on when a world-famous writer suddenly decides to stop writing? *(Shakes his head)* You're making a big mistake.

ROGER *(Irritated):* Good grief, Bernie. Stop being such a pessimist. Our plan's worked so far, hasn't it?

BERNIE *(Upset):* For you, sure. You're the one with your name up in lights.

ROGER *(Patting* BERNIE *on the shoulder):* Ah, the perils of being a ghostwriter! But look at the bright side: This arrangement's kept your great uncle's house from being sold, hasn't it?

BERNIE: But you've been passing off the house as yours.

ROGER *(Sighing):* I don't see what you're complaining about. In two more weeks, we can go our separate ways and you can write to your heart's content.

BERNIE: But nobody's even heard of me!

ROGER: True. But then, no one had heard of me either until you came along with all those stories about pirates and plunder.

BERNIE: Stories? They happen to be from real life.

My great uncle's life, to be precise. Besides, you told me you only wanted help getting started.

ROGER: So?

BERNIE: So I've been helping you get started for seven years, and not once have I seen you touch that typewriter.

ROGER *(Leaning over and dramatically touching typewriter):* There! I've touched it—are you satisfied?

BERNIE: Roger—

ROGER *(Glancing at watch):* Listen, Bernie, I'd love to continue this, but Cynthia's due any second, and I have to start lunch.

BERNIE: Good. I'd like to meet her.

ROGER: Maybe at the wedding. For now, how about taking the rest of the day off?

BERNIE: Why?

ROGER: Because I want everything to go perfectly.

BERNIE: In other words, you're afraid I'll tell her that you're planning to retire from writing and live off her fortune?

ROGER: Exactly. Besides, I want her to have every opportunity to look around and enjoy the house. She's a romantic, you know.

BERNIE: Oh, really?

ROGER: Ships, mansions, ghosts—that sort of thing. *(Moving left toward exit)* She's read every one of my books, by the way.

BERNIE: *My* books, you mean. (ROGER *exits.* BERNIE *picks up some manuscripts from desk.)* I suppose I can't complain, though. I wouldn't have even a house if the books hadn't been best sellers. *(Sighs deeply)* Well, behind every great writer, there's a talented but obscure ghostwriter. I just wish I were the one out in front. *(Noise is heard from hallway.)* Here they come! I guess that's my cue not to stand in the way of true romance. . . . *(Steps behind curtains right, as* CYNTHIA *and* ROGER *enter)*

ROGER *(Waving his hand grandly):* Come in and make yourself at home, Cynthia.

CYNTHIA: So this is where you get your inspiration, Roger?

ROGER: Actually, I get most of my inspiration *(Turning to face her)* from just looking in your eyes.

CYNTHIA *(Smiling):* Oh, Roger, you say the most romantic things . . . just like the characters in your books! *(During this conversation,* BERNIE *looks on in amusement from behind curtain.)*

ROGER: I'm glad you think so. . . . How do you like the house?

CYNTHIA: A little on the musty side . . . but it has a certain charm.

ROGER: It's about a hundred years old. It was built by Phineas Drake.

CYNTHIA *(Surprised):* The pirate captain in your stories?

ROGER: The very same. The house was an absolute steal. (BERNIE *nods.)*

CYNTHIA: I don't see how you could bear to sell it. Did you talk to the real estate woman I recommended? (BERNIE *pokes his head out;* ROGER *sees him.*)

ROGER *(Anxiously, as he takes her arm):* Uh— maybe we should talk about it in the kitchen.

CYNTHIA: Why can't we talk about it here?

ROGER: Oh, you know what they say . . . about the walls having ears?

CYNTHIA *(Laughing):* Are you saying Crumbling Gables has ghosts?

ROGER *(Quickly):* Yes, of course—didn't I tell you?

CYNTHIA: How exciting! I'd love to meet one—especially Captain Drake himself!

ROGER *(Uneasily):* Yes, well, I'm sure he's still hanging around. *(Guides her toward exit)* Drake's picture is out in the hall—go take a look. I'll join you in just a minute. *(She exits.* BERNIE *comes out from behind curtain.)*

BERNIE *(Annoyed):* Did you tell Cynthia you were going to sell *my* house?

ROGER: I can explain, Bernie.

BERNIE *(Angrily):* So can I. To Cynthia. *(Starts toward door)*

ROGER *(Blocking his path):* Well, we couldn't very well move in with you living here, too.

BERNIE: You're really planning to sell it?

ROGER: Well—yes and no. I mean, I'm selling it to you, Bernie.

BERNIE: But I already own it.

ROGER: Yes, I know that, but I have to make Cynthia think—*(Quickly)* Quiet—she's coming back. We'll talk later. *(Pushes* BERNIE *behind curtains, just as* CYNTHIA *enters)*

CYNTHIA *(Sighing):* Captain Drake is just as I imagined him. I almost expected him to jump right out of the picture and sweep me off my feet!

ROGER: You're making me jealous. *(Smiles)* Well, I won't have to worry—he's been dead for a good hundred years.

CYNTHIA: What happened to him?

ROGER: Lost at sea, I imagine. *(Shrugs)* Occupational hazard of being a pirate.

CYNTHIA *(Curiously):* Did he ever marry?

ROGER *(Amused):* You're taking an unusual amount of interest in someone fictional, aren't you, Cynthia?

CYNTHIA: Fictional? Nonsense! You said he was a real person.

ROGER: True. But the magic of these fingers *(Wiggling them)* at the typewriter added the glamour and excitement to an otherwise uninspiring life. *(Checks watch)* I should get started on our lunch. Want to help?

CYNTHIA *(Looking around):* Do you mind if I stay in here for awhile, Roger? *(Kissing him on cheek)* I feel that I'll know you much better just by soaking up all the vibrations from this room.

ROGER *(Reluctantly):* All right, if you want to. *(Louder, toward curtains, so* BERNIE *can hear)*

But I'll be right back! *(Exits;* CYNTHIA *wanders around room, looking at everything. Her glance settles on manuscript that* BERNIE *left on desk.)*

CYNTHIA *(Picking up manuscript):* Why, this must be the new manuscript Roger told me he was working on. *(Opens it to the middle and starts to read out loud)* "The sunset was one of pink and gold. The lonely silhouette of his handsome profile faced the open sea, each day of the journey taking him farther from Penelope's side. She was his one, true love, the woman he valued more than the ransoms of kings whose ships he plundered."

ROGER *(Returning, carrying glass of iced tea):* I'm back! (CYNTHIA *jumps, startled.)* Sorry—I didn't mean to startle you.

CYNTHIA: I was so engrossed in the story, I didn't hear you come in.

ROGER *(Handing her the tea):* The new manuscript is still pretty rough, but *(Smugly)* like my other books, I'm sure it'll make the bestseller list. It almost wrote itself. . . .

CYNTHIA *(Impressed):* I just can't get over what a wonderful imagination you have, Roger. Do you really think the ghost is still around?

ROGER: Whose ghost?

CYNTHIA: Captain Drake's, of course.

ROGER *(Warily):* I suppose so. Why?

CYNTHIA: Well, they say that ghosts haunt places only if they have unfinished business.

ROGER: Such as?

CYNTHIA: Oh, I don't know. A lost treasure, perhaps? Or unrequited love? (BERNIE *tiptoes out of room behind them.*)

ROGER: Speaking of imagination, Cynthia, I think you're getting carried away. He's just a figment of my imagination.

CYNTHIA *(Dreamily):* Yes, but he's my kind of hero—so vibrant, so lifelike, so wonderful!

ROGER *(Putting his arm around her):* I think your imagination could be put to better use planning our wedding!

CYNTHIA: I hope your feelings won't be hurt, Roger, but would you mind if we talked about the wedding plans after lunch? I'd really like to get back to the story!

ROGER: The light in the kitchen is much better for reading. *(Tries to lead her toward exit)*

CYNTHIA *(Breaking away):* No problem. *(Crosses to curtains)* I'll just open these curtains.

ROGER *(Trying to hold her back):* No! *(She opens curtains. BERNIE is gone. CYNTHIA turns to ROGER, puzzled. He shrugs.)* No problem about the light; you're right. I'll go see about lunch. *(Exits)*

CYNTHIA *(Picking up manuscript again, reading):* "They were destined to meet again one day, their lips to touch, the fragrance of gardenias in her hair." *(As she reads, BERNIE quietly enters, now dressed like Captain Drake. She continues read-*

ing.) "Her letters sustained him in his loneliness. He read them a thousand times each evening by the candlelight of his cabin, dreaming of the day he would return to her, when she would run into his arms and say—"

BERNIE *(With an English accent):* I've missed you. (CYNTHIA *jumps, frightened.* BERNIE *bows gallantly to her.)* Forgiveness I beg of you, dear lady, if I caused you fright.

CYNTHIA: Who are you?

BERNIE: Is my face unfamiliar?

CYNTHIA *(Taking a closer look, shaking her head in disbelief):* No, it can't be! I don't believe it.

BERNIE *(Sighing):* That's what they all say.

CYNTHIA: It's incredible—you look just like *(Pointing to hallway)* the man in the picture. Captain Phineas Drake.

BERNIE: Perhaps I do . . . because I am.

CYNTHIA: But you're—

BERNIE: Yes, I'm afraid so. I'm a ghost.

CYNTHIA *(Alarmed):* But that's impossible! I can see you!

BERNIE: Of course . . . because I want you to.

CYNTHIA *(Pleased):* You do?

BERNIE: Your spirit is gentle, your charm a welcome delight. *(Sincerely)* I feel you can be trusted.

CYNTHIA: Can Roger see you, too?

BERNIE *(Quickly; shaking his head):* No, not at all.

He's quite busy with his writing, you see.

CYNTHIA (*Studying him a moment*): Is something wrong?

BERNIE (*Dramatically*): Only an ache of the heart, dear lady—one that compels me forever to haunt these halls until the proper conditions have been met.

CYNTHIA: Conditions? What conditions?

BERNIE: Oh, I wouldn't want to bother you with my troubles. (*Shrugs*) I might as well just walk back through the wall.

CYNTHIA: No, please, wait! I'd like to help if I could.

BERNIE (*Sighing*): There's really nothing that anyone can do. You see, when I was lost at sea, my body was never found.

CYNTHIA: Oh, dear!

BERNIE: And I must haunt Crumbling Gables until I can prove that I am indeed no longer among the living. (*Dramatically*) Or until—

CYNTHIA: Or until what?

BERNIE (*Slowly*): Or until someone falls in love with me.

CYNTHIA: But you're a ghost. How could anyone fall in love with you?

BERNIE (*Sighing*): That is the problem. The only way that people know about me is through Roger Bridesmith's novels. Even then, though, they think I'm nothing more than a figment of his imagination.

CYNTHIA *(Protesting):* But you seem so real! So exciting!

BERNIE: Compliments are sweet to my ear, but only the proper words—spoken from the heart—would restore me to the here and now.

CYNTHIA *(With growing interest):* What do you mean?

BERNIE: It's really quite simple. If a member of the fair sex were to say that she was in love with me, I'd be allowed to come back to life. Not as I am, of course. But in the form of someone else—perhaps someone even ordinary and unassuming.

CYNTHIA: That's really all it would take?

BERNIE: Yes—but alas, it's an impossibility.

CYNTHIA: But how would I—I mean, how would she know that it was you?

BERNIE *(Smiling at her):* Looking in the eyes, they say, is how you know. Just as I knew when you were looking up at my picture. For a moment you reminded me of someone. Someone named Penelope. *(Sighs)* Well, I suppose I've taken enough of your time.

CYNTHIA: Don't leave.

BERNIE: I really should. If Mr. Bridesmith were to come in and see you talking to yourself, I daresay he'd worry about you.

CYNTHIA: But he'd be so thrilled that you were haunting his house that—

BERNIE: No, I don't think so—and I wouldn't mention anything about this to him if I were you.

CYNTHIA *(Reluctantly):* Well, if you insist. *(Holds out her hand)*

BERNIE *(Looking at it, sadly):* Much as I'd like to take your hand in mine, dear lady, you would be shaking thin air.

CYNTHIA: Oh, yes, of course, I forgot. *(Smiles; hopefully)* Perhaps we'll meet again some time?

BERNIE: One never knows. *(Exits)*

CYNTHIA *(In amazement):* To think that he was actually here! That I actually saw him . . . talked to him!

ROGER *(Re-entering):* Cynthia! Whom are you talking to?

CYNTHIA *(Quickly):* No one! No one at all, Roger. I was just reading aloud from your manuscript.

ROGER: Well, that's good. I'd worry about you if you were talking to ghosts or something. *(Holding out his hand)* Ready for lunch?

CYNTHIA *(Walking away from him):* Actually, I've been thinking, Roger.

ROGER *(Following her):* Thinking about our wedding, I'd wager?

CYNTHIA: Yes. Yes, I have.

ROGER: Good. So have I. What have you been thinking?

CYNTHIA *(Turning to face him):* I've been thinking, Roger, that you're a wonderful person, and you have lots of nice qualities . . . not to mention lots of talent.

ROGER: True.

CYNTHIA: But I just can't go ahead with our marriage!

ROGER *(Stunned):* What are you talking about?

CYNTHIA: There isn't an easy way to tell you this, Roger, but I think I'm in love with someone else.

ROGER: Someone else? Who? Where did you meet him—and when?

CYNTHIA: Actually, he's someone you introduced me to.

ROGER: But I haven't introduced you to anyone!

CYNTHIA: Through your books you have.

ROGER *(Puzzled):* What do you mean?

CYNTHIA: I'm in love with Captain Drake! (ROGER *laughs.*) What's so funny?

ROGER: Your falling in love with someone in a book. That's the most ridiculous thing I've ever heard! (BERNIE *enters, dressed again as he was at the start of the play, carrying some file folders.*)

BERNIE: Excuse me. (CYNTHIA *stares at him.*)

ROGER: In a minute, Bernie, we're—*(Does a doubletake)* Bernie! What are you doing here?

BERNIE: Sorry to interrupt you, Mr. Bridesmith, but I finished that research you asked me to do at the library, and I thought—*(Smiles at* CYNTHIA*)* Hello.

CYNTHIA *(Extending her hand):* Hello. I'm Cynthia Crutsinger.

BERNIE: I'm Bernie. *(Shakes her hand; turns)* About the research, Mr. Bridesmith—?

ROGER *(Moving to step between the two of them):*

I'm sure it's fine. (BERNIE *and* CYNTHIA *stare at each other.*)

CYNTHIA (*To* BERNIE): Have we met before?

BERNIE: I'm sure I would have remembered if we had, Miss Crutsinger.

CYNTHIA *(Puzzled):* There's something so familiar about you—

ROGER *(Clearing throat):* Don't you have to be running along, Bernie? Miss Crutsinger and I were just about to have lunch.

CYNTHIA: Actually, I really should be running along myself, Roger. (*To* BERNIE) Could I give you a lift, Bernie?

BERNIE: Well, I have a lot of work to do, and—

CYNTHIA *(Ignoring* ROGER *completely):* Lunch, then? Maybe in an hour at the Crow's Nest?

BERNIE *(Surprised):* Sure. Yes, lunch sounds fine.

ROGER *(Upset):* Cynthia!

CYNTHIA (*To* ROGER): I'm sorry things didn't work out, Roger. But don't worry, your ship will come in someday, and you'll meet someone wonderful on it.

ROGER: Cynthia, what are you saying?

CYNTHIA: See you in an hour, Bernie?

BERNIE: Sure. See you then. (CYNTHIA *exits.*)

ROGER *(Upset):* I don't understand. (*To* BERNIE) Everything was fine a few minutes ago!

BERNIE *(Shrugging):* You can't win 'em all, Roger.

ROGER: What do I do now, Bernie?

BERNIE: Well, for starters *(Handing him folders),*

you could learn how to write. It's time to go our separate ways.

ROGER: I can't believe this is happening to me. *(Exits.* BERNIE *chuckles, starts to exit, pauses a moment and looks around room.)*

BERNIE: Thanks, Uncle Phineas.

VOICE *(Recording of* BERNIE'S *voice, with English accent, echoing and ghostlike):* Anytime, Bernie. Anytime at all. *(Chuckles; curtain)*

THE END

PRODUCTON NOTES

GHOSTWRITER OR GHOST?

Characters: 2 male; 1 female.

Playing Time: 15 minutes.

Costumes: Slacks, shirt, tie for Roger; jeans, sweater, sneakers, glasses and pirate costume for Bernie; dress or skirt and sweater for Cynthia.

Properties: Books; papers; ice tea glass.

Setting: Library with desk, bookcases and chairs. Papers and type-writer are on desk. Curtains are down right. Artifacts from old sailing ships round out the decor.

Lighting and Sound: Taped voice for final line of play.

A Rose Is Just a Rose

Characters

PEMBERTON, *lab assistant*
DR. IRVING SMEDLAP, *renowned scientist*
DIANA, *lab assistant*
WILLIAM SHAKESPEARE
BILL, *lab assistant*

TIME: *The present.*
SETTING: *Dr. Irving Smedlap's laboratory, cluttered with electronic gadgets, scientific equipment, papers on counters and shelves. Entrance to lab is left; large refrigerator-size box—Dr. Smedlap's invention, the Time Mobile—stands at right.*
AT RISE: PEMBERTON, *agitated, bursts into lab, followed closely by an angry* DR. SMEDLAP.
PEMBERTON *(Upset):* It was an accident, Dr. Smedlap! I swear it was! *(Pointing at the ma-*

chine) He was standing right there when it happened.

SMEDLAP: Near the Time Mobile?

PEMBERTON: No, sir. *(Wincing) In* the Time Mobile.

SMEDLAP *(Angrily):* Pemberton, I've said it a thousand times—(PEMBERTON *repeats the next sentence along with* SMEDLAP.) Absolutely *no one* tests the Time Mobile until it's ready.

PEMBERTON: Yes, I know, sir. And Bill knew that, too, but—

SMEDLAP: Then what was he doing in the Time Mobile?

PEMBERTON: Checking out a noise from inside the machine.

SMEDLAP: Impossible! The machine is empty!

PEMBERTON: That's what I said, but he insisted on taking a look. Next thing I knew, the door slammed shut behind him.

SMEDLAP: Why didn't you open it and tell him to come back out?

PEMBERTON: It was sealed tight. (SMEDLAP *crosses to machine*.) So tight that there wasn't any way I—(SMEDLAP *opens door easily to reveal an empty box.)* Gosh! How did you do that?

DIANA *(Entering):* What's going on? *(Looks around)* Where's Bill?

PEMBERTON: He's gone, Diana. *(Hastily)* But don't ask me where.

DIANA: Stop clowning around, Pemberton. Where is he?

SMEDLAP: What he's trying to say, Diana, is that Bill has gone for an unauthorized trip—*(Pointing to machine)* in there.

DIANA: But that's impossible.

PEMBERTON: It was an accident, Diana. I tried to get him out, but he was lost before I could get the door open.

DIANA *(Upset):* Lost? Lost where?

SMEDLAP: Somewhere in time . . . if the machine worked properly, that is.

PEMBERTON: I'm really sorry, Diana. I mean, since you had a crush on him and all . . .

DIANA *(Indignantly):* I most certainly did not! Why would I have a crush on someone who always has his nose in a book?

PEMBERTON *(Shrugging):* Opposites attract?

SMEDLAP *(Sarcastically):* May we please dispense with advice to the lovelorn? *(They look at him.)* We have a serious problem on our hands.

PEMBERTON: Right. We've got to get Bill back.

SMEDLAP: More important, Pemberton, we've got to get someone here to take his place in the 20th century.

DIANA: Why do we have to do that?

SMEDLAP: Because Bill—without even knowing it— has just upset the molecular balance of our entire history with his little junket to a different century. If he has traveled back to a different time, the universe is now faced with the awesome dilemma of having one more person in it than it had before.

PEMBERTON: Well, gee, it's not as if he's going to eat a lot or anything . . .

SMEDLAP: True, but he could do something that will have a drastic effect on the future. That's why we have to balance his absence in this century with a presence from a past century.

PEMBERTON: But what if we get someone like Attila the Hun? *(Shakes his head)* I really don't think he'd fit into our society very well—running all amuck and creating confusion!

DIANA *(Snapping fingers):* Oh, that reminds me, Dr. Smedlap. I came to tell you that I've got Washington on the phone . . .

SMEDLAP: Hm-m-m. . . . I guess I'd better take it. *(Starts to exit)* Don't touch anything while I'm gone, Pemberton! *(Exits, followed by* DIANA*)*

PEMBERTON *(Sighing):* I've really done it this time! *(Looks up and around room)* I don't know where you've gone, Bill, but right now I sure wish I could join you. *(Shakes head)* I'll be lucky if I still have a job tomorrow. *(As he speaks, door of machine opens and* WILLIAM SHAKESPEARE *emerges cautiously. He wears tights, pantaloons and white shirt.)* I seem to make things happen even when I'm doing nothing!

WILLIAM *(Putting hand in front of eyes, as if blinded by lights):* Hark! What light from yonder window breaks?

PEMBERTON: Terrific. Now I'm even hearing voices.

WILLIAM *(Snapping fingers):* You, lad—a word with you!

PEMBERTON *(Noticing him; alarmed):* Hey—what are you doing in here? *(Rushing up to him)* This is a top-secret lab—nobody's allowed in here! *(Hustling him to door of lab)*

WILLIAM: Indeed, good fellow? *(Looking around in amazement)* Do mine eyes deceive me? Or in life's fleeting moment, have I traversed to a land foreign and strange?

PEMBERTON: You're in Los Angeles. And we're both in big trouble if you don't get out of here.

WILLIAM *(Curiously):* Speak the speech, then, I pray you, trippingly upon the tongue.

PEMBERTON: Look, there's no time for speeches, mister. *(Opening lab door)* There's the front door. I don't want to catch you back in here again, understand?

WILLIAM *(Puzzled):* What folly is this?

PEMBERTON: It's no folly at all. Out! *(Pushes* WILLIAM *off and closes door behind him. Shakes his head)* I wonder who that was? I feel as if I know him from somewhere.

SMEDLAP *(Entering brusquely):* All right, Pemberton. I'll need you to take notes on this.

PEMBERTON: Yes, sir. *(Picks up paper and pen)*

SMEDLAP: Didn't touch anything while I was gone, did you?

PEMBERTON: No, sir.

SMEDLAP: Well, that's good. *(Crossing to look at machine closely)*

DIANA *(Entering, somewhat dreamily, holding a red rose):* I just met the most charming man in the hallway.

SMEDLAP *(Suspiciously):* Man? What man?

DIANA: I don't know. He was dressed rather strangely, but—

SMEDLAP: You've never seen him before?

DIANA: Not that I recall. *(Smiles)* He had the most wonderful manners, though . . .

SMEDLAP *(Sighing heavily):* I'd better call Security. *(Exits)*

DIANA: He said the cutest thing—"A rose by any other name—"

PEMBERTON *(Nervously):* Diana—

DIANA *(Knowingly):* I just love a man who can quote Shakespeare.

PEMBERTON *(Suddenly):* Oh, my gosh! That's it! *(Runs out)*

DIANA: I wonder what he's so flustered about. *(Sniffs rose)* I'd better put this in water so it will last. *(Strolls out)*

PEMBERTON *(Entering a moment later with a very confused WILLIAM):* Sorry I chased you out before. I just didn't realize who you were.

WILLIAM: What manner of magic is this, sir, that my

name be known and yet our acquaintance a
puzzlement to me?

PEMBERTON: Everyone's heard of you! You're
William Shakespeare, and you're famous!

WILLIAM *(Incredulously):* Famous? Verily have I
wished to grasp such fortune, but alas! He who
steals my purse finds very little within.

PEMBERTON: You mean . . . you're out of ideas?

WILLIAM *(Nodding):* 'Tis the slings and arrows of
outrageous fortune that have struck their mark
. . . and quelled my spirit.

PEMBERTON: Look . . . everybody has a bad day
now and then.

WILLIAM *(Shaking his head):* Something is rotten in
the state of Denmark.

PEMBERTON *(Pleased):* Hey, I know that one! It's
from *Hamlet!*

WILLIAM *(Puzzled): Hamlet?* What's that?

PEMBERTON: You mean you don't remember your
own play?

WILLIAM: Sir, your words be riddles to me.

PEMBERTON: Well, what about *Julius Caesar?
Romeo and Juliet?* And *King Lear?*

WILLIAM *(Stopping him):* Should I know these people?

PEMBERTON: Of course! They're all characters from
your plays.

WILLIAM: Truly you have mistaken me for another, a
countryman perhaps?

PEMBERTON: Don't be ridiculous! *(Suddenly)* Uh-oh.

WILLIAM: What manner of speech is "uh-oh"? Your face, my friend, betrays an error of tragic consequence.

PEMBERTON: I just realized that you don't know what I'm talking about because none of it has happened yet. (WILLIAM *looks at him in confusion.*) This is going to be hard to explain, but this friend of mine stepped into that machine *(Points)* by accident, and—

WILLIAM *(Turning to look at it):* How strange! From whence did it come?

PEMBERTON: Oh, we built it right here in the lab. It's called a Time Mobile, and it moves people from one period of time to another. . . . Is any of this making sense? (WILLIAM *shakes his head.*) I guess what I'm trying to say is that you're not supposed to be here.

WILLIAM: To be or not to be, that is the question. *(Thinking)* I was sitting at my desk, quill in hand, set to write a sonnet to my lady, and suddenly I find myself in this *(Gesturing)* unfamiliar place.

SMEDLAP *(Loudly; offstage):* Well, he's gone now, whoever he was!

PEMBERTON *(Alarmed; pushing* WILLIAM *into Time Mobile):* Quick, in here! *(Closes door of Time Mobile)* And don't say a word! (SMEDLAP *and* DIANA *enter.*)

SMEDLAP: Now then, where was I?

PEMBERTON *(Suddenly):* Gosh—*(Looking at his watch)* look at the time!

DIANA *(Checking her watch):* What about it, Pemberton?

PEMBERTON: Why, it's time for lunch! *(Crossing to* DIANA *and throwing his arm around her shoulder)* How about lunch on me, you two?

DIANA *(Sarcastically):* Lunch on you, Pemberton, means Mr. Milkshake. I think I'll pass.

SMEDLAP: Thanks, Pemberton, but I have work to do. *(Crosses to machine)*

PEMBERTON *(Rushing after him):* Uh—is that your phone I hear ringing, Dr. Smedlap?

SMEDLAP: I don't hear anything.

DIANA: Neither do I.

PEMBERTON: Wait—there it is again. Yes, sir, I'd say it's definitely your phone. It could be an emergency.

SMEDLAP *(Crossing to door):* I don't know what's wrong with you, Pemberton. You're acting so strange today. *(Exits)*

PEMBERTON *(To* DIANA): Don't you think you should go with him?

DIANA *(Puzzled):* What for?

PEMBERTON: Well, you never know. It could be an emergency that takes two people to solve.

DIANA *(Annoyed):* Are you trying to get rid of me, Pemberton?

PEMBERTON: Why would I want to do that? *(Sud-*

denly) By the way, did you find out who left the box of candy on your desk?

DIANA: What box of candy?

PEMBERTON: At least I think it was for you. Big heart-shaped box with a red ribbon and lace and—

DIANA: I'll go take a look. *(She exits. PEMBERTON runs over to machine and opens door.)*

PEMBERTON: Come on out, William. We've got to hide you someplace else until I can figure out how to get you back to your own time. *(They cross to lab door, which is immediately opened by SMEDLAP.)*

SMEDLAP: Your ears are playing tricks, Pemberton. I didn't—

PEMBERTON *(Startled):* Hello, Dr. Smedlap. *(Takes WILLIAM's arm)* Say, Dr. Smedlap, have you ever met . . . *(Hastily)* my brother? William, Dr. Smedlap. Dr. Smedlap, William *(Starts to exit)* Sorry we have to run, but—

SMEDLAP *(Sternly):* Pemberton. You know the rules. No one's allowed in the lab except personnel cleared by Security.

PEMBERTON: Exactly, sir. That's why we were just leaving, sir. You see, William stopped by to join me for lunch.

DIANA *(Entering; annoyed):* Pemberton, I've looked all over and I can't find any—*(Stops, smiles when she sees WILLIAM)* Well, we meet again!

WILLIAM *(Taking her hand and kissing it):* Parting was such sweet sorrow.

PEMBERTON: And parting is exactly what we have to do. *(Rushing him to door)*

DIANA: Pemberton, aren't you going to introduce us?

PEMBERTON: Uh—sure. William, Diana. Diana, my cousin William.

SMEDLAP *(Puzzled):* I thought you said he was your brother.

PEMBERTON: Did I? Silly me. Actually we're cousins, but we've always been like brothers. Close family, you know. *(Hastily)* See you after lunch! *(He and* WILLIAM *rush out.)*

SMEDLAP *(Shaking head):* That Pemberton certainly is a weird character! *(Quick curtain)*

*   *   *   *   *

SCENE 2

TIME: *An hour later.*

SETTING: *Same.*

AT RISE: PEMBERTON *and* WILLIAM *enter, finishing milkshakes.*

PEMBERTON: We're in luck! They're gone. Now, if my theory is right, all I have to do is set the dials for the date and time you gave me and send you back to Stratford-on-Avon. With luck, you'll be back in time for dinner.

WILLIAM *(Concerned):* What of your friend Bill?

PEMBERTON *(Shrugging):* Who knows? Maybe you passed each other in time, in which case your going back may bump him back into the present and everything will be fine. That is, I think everything will be fine.

WILLIAM: Verily do I long for my own hearth. *(Shivers)* I left my coat behind.

PEMBERTON *(Checking his watch):* We'd better hurry—I've got to get you back to England so you can get on with becoming famous.

WILLIAM *(Sighing):* Would that it be so! If in sleep I were perchance to dream, then plots aplenty might reveal themselves to me. And I should then take up my quill and write words witty and bold.

PEMBERTON: Exactly!

WILLIAM *(Looking around):* But on the other hand, a change of century might do me well. This one, perchance—

PEMBERTON *(In a panic):* But you can't! I mean, this is a nice place to visit, but there just isn't any way you can stay here!

WILLIAM: Is your world so unpleasant, then?

PEMBERTON: No, actually, it's pretty good. Lots of things to do around here—like Disneyland and computer games and old movies on the VCR . . .

WILLIAM: Movies?

PEMBERTON: Yeah, that's something you could probably get into, being a writer, and all. My all-time favorite is *Casablanca. (Starts to sing)* "You must remember this, a kiss is still a kiss . . ."

WILLIAM *(Joining in):* "A rose is just a rose. . . ."

PEMBERTON: Listen, I've got to get you out of here before they come back and start asking questions.

WILLIAM: But wait! A plot or two from the tales of which you speak so fondly might set me in a new direction.

PEMBERTON *(Thinking for a moment):* I guess there's no harm in telling you about them. Let me see—*Romeo and Juliet* is about these two families, the Montagues and the Capulets. They really hate each other but the two lovers want to get married.

WILLIAM: And happily shall they dwell ever after?

PEMBERTON: Actually, no. You see, that's the whole point of the plays you wrote . . . or, I should say, that you're going to write when you get back.

WILLIAM: Hm-m. And Hamlet—what of him?

PEMBERTON: He's this young prince who talks to the ghost of his father and finds out that his evil uncle murdered his father, married his mother, and took over the kingdom.

WILLIAM: How intriguing this is! Has Hamlet an interest in romance?

PEMBERTON: Well, Ophelia is really crazy about him, but he hardly seems to notice her. Sort of like Bill and Diana.

WILLIAM: Bill and Diana? Did I write about them, too?

PEMBERTON: No, Bill and Diana are real people. And—oh, never mind. What else now? *(Thinking)*

Then there's Macbeth—witches, murder, power, trees advancing on Dunsinaine. Really commercial stuff.

WILLIAM: Trees advancing on Dunsinaine? What work of sorcery is this?

PEMBERTON: Oh, none at all, just a clever twist— you had the soldiers hold branches up to their faces and move up and attack the castle.

WILLIAM *(Excitedly):* Marvelous, yes! I can see it now!

PEMBERTON: Is that enough to get you going?

WILLIAM *(Bowing):* With infinite gratitude, I bid you adieu.

PEMBERTON *(Opening door of machine):* Have a nice trip, and don't forget to write! *(Closes door, pushes a few buttons. Machine starts to make loud noise.* SMEDLAP *and* DIANA *enter.)*

SMEDLAP: Pemberton! I told you not to touch anything!

PEMBERTON *(Quickly withdrawing handkerchief from pocket and pretending to dust):* Just dusting, sir.

SMEDLAP: Well, why don't you dust somewhere else? I don't want you to push anything by accident and cause a catastrophe!

PEMBERTON: Yes, sir.

DIANA *(Looking around):* Did William leave already?

PEMBERTON: William? Uh, yeah, he had to get home.

DIANA: I liked him a lot. Does he always dress that way?

PEMBERTON: What way?

DIANA: Like an extra in a Shakespearean tragedy?

PEMBERTON *(Shrugging):* Part of his charm, I guess.

SMEDLAP *(Annoyed):* Would anyone mind if we got back to work? *(Pauses)* Now, as I was saying, Diana—*(Knocking sound comes from within machine.)* What was that?

PEMBERTON *(Quickly):* I didn't hear it.

DIANA: Hear what?

PEMBERTON: Whatever it was that Dr. Smedlap thought he heard but didn't. *(Knocking sound is heard again.)*

SMEDLAP: There it is again.

PEMBERTON: No, it isn't.

DIANA: It's coming from inside the machine!

PEMBERTON *(Laughing nervously):* Don't be ridiculous! How could anything be making noise in the machine when all of us know the machine is empty?

DIANA *(Suspiciously):* How do we know it's empty?

SMEDLAP: I'd better take a look. *(Moves to machine)*

PEMBERTON *(Blocking door of machine):* Are you sure you want to do that, sir? It could be dangerous!

SMEDLAP: Nonsense! Something or someone is in there, and I want to know what it is! (PEMBERTON *steps back, and* SMEDLAP *flings open ma-*

chine door. BILL *comes out. He is wearing modern clothes except for a Shakespearean jacket. He carries a quill in one hand and a piece of parchment in the other.)* Bill!

DIANA *(Delighted):* Bill! I'm so glad to see you.

PEMBERTON *(Tentatively):* Bill?

SMEDLAP *(Firmly):* You've got some explaining to do, young man.

BILL *(Blinking in confusion):* Dr. Smedlap? Diana? Pemberton?

SMEDLAP *(Sternly):* Don't play games with us, Bill. I want to know exactly where you've been.

BILL *(Bewildered):* I wish I knew exactly where I've been myself.

DIANA: What are you talking about?

BILL: The last thing I remember was walking into the Time Mobile and then the next thing I knew, I was sitting in a thatched cottage in the country.

DIANA *(Taking parchment from him):* What's this? A note?

BILL: I don't know. Something I must have been writing before I fell asleep. (DIANA *reads it to herself.)* I was really tired, so I put my head down on the desk and when I woke up, I was back here.

DIANA: Oh, Bill, it's the most beautiful poem I've ever read. *(Coyly)* Did you really mean it?

BILL *(Confused):* Sure . . . uh, I guess so.

PEMBERTON: Where did you get that jacket, Bill?

BILL: It was hanging on the back of the chair. I got cold, so I put it on.

DIANA *(Throwing her arms around him):* Bill, I'm

so happy you're back!

SMEDLAP: Enough of this romantic nonsense! This is a serious lab, and we have serious experiments to do. (*To* BILL) If you hadn't come back from your coffee break when you did, young man, we could have upset the entire course of history!

BILL (*Puzzled*): Coffee break?

SMEDLAP (*To* DIANA): I'll be in my office, Diana. And I don't want to be interrupted unless it's a genuine emergency. (*Exits*)

DIANA (*As she exits with* BILL): Oh, Bill, I was so worried about you!

BILL (*With broad smile*): You were?

DIANA: Here we all thought that we had lost you somewhere in time, and it turns out you were safe as could be!

BILL: I guess so.

DIANA: And I just adore the poem—it's so original! (*They exit.* PEMBERTON *watches them go, then crosses to machine. He scratches his head, then opens the door and peers inside. He closes it and makes perplexed gesture as the curtains close.*)

THE END

PRODUCTION NOTES

A Rose Is Just a Rose

Characters: 4 *male; 1 female.*

Playing Time: 15 minutes.

Costumes: Pemberton, Smedlap and Diana wear white lab coats over regular clothes; William is dressed in Shakespearean clothes; Bill wears modern clothes and Shakespearean jacket. Pemberton has handkerchief in pocket.

Properties: Paper; pen; red rose; two milkshakes; parchment; quill pen.

Setting: Laboratory with high counters and shelves, piled high with test tubes, microscopes, papers, etc. Entrance to lab is left; large refrigerator-sized box—the Time Mobile—is right.

Lighting and Sound: No special effects.

Lessons of Oz

Characters

DOROTHY OSBOURNE, *a celebrated novelist*
MS. JANE FRITZ, *librarian*
SCARECROW
TIN WOODMAN } *Dorothy's friends*
COWARDLY LION
LETITIA SHARPE, *a teacher*
PROFESSOR, *a mysterious visitor*
FOUR READERS, *Dorothy's fans*

TIME: *The present.*
SETTING: *The Topeka, Kansas, Public Library. Desk and chair are down left. An easel with poster showing book that reads* KANSAS NEVER LOOKED SO GOOD, BY DOROTHY OSBOURNE, *is at right. Curtain hangs behind desk. Table piled with books is next to working door, up center. Backdrop shows stacks of books.*

AT RISE: MS. JANE FRITZ *sits at desk.* DOROTHY *enters right, carrying a basket with a stuffed dog in it.* MS. FRITZ *rises to greet her.*

MS. FRITZ *(Enthusiastically):* Welcome, Dorothy. I just can't tell you how thrilled we are to have you here to autograph your books for our readers! *(Pointing to basket)* And I see you have your little dog with you.

DOROTHY *(Crossing to desk):* Yes, Toto and I have been pretty busy on the lecture circuit these days.

MS. FRITZ: Well, the next three weeks will just fly by before you know it.

DOROTHY *(Startled):* Three weeks?

MS. FRITZ: Of course! Nearly everyone within shouting distance of Topeka has bought your new novel, Miss Osbourne. Now, I've figured out on my computer that fifteen seconds per autograph in a twelve-hour day, with a half hour for lunch and an afternoon break for tea—

DOROTHY *(Upset):* Do you expect me to sit here and autograph books for three weeks?

MS. FRITZ: We can't disappoint your fans, can we, Miss Osbourne? Here's a pen for you. *(Hands her pen)* And here they come now. (FOUR READERS *enter, one by one, through door center.)* Happy signing. *(Turns to greet* READERS)

DOROTHY *(Sitting; as if talking to dog in basket):* I guess those chores for Auntie Em will have to wait, Toto. (READERS *pick up copies of book from table by door, then line up at desk.* SCARECROW *and* TIN WOODMAN *enter, join line.* SCARECROW, *who hides his face with a book, is third in line,* TIN WOODMAN *fifth.*)

1ST READER *(Setting book in front of* DOROTHY): I just loved your new book, Miss Osbourne. (DOROTHY *smiles and nods pleasantly.*)

DOROTHY: Thank you. *(Signs book)*

1ST READER: It was so real, so moving, so deep.

DOROTHY *(Handing book back):* I'm glad you enjoyed it. (1ST READER *exits.*)

2ND READER *(Stepping up to desk):* Oh, Miss Osbourne, I can't tell you what a fan of yours I am. *(Passes book to her)*

DOROTHY *(Nodding pleasantly):* How nice of you! *(Signs book)*

2ND READER: As a matter of fact, I have a few ideas of my own that my friends say would make a wonderful book. Or even a movie.

DOROTHY: Yes, I'm sure they would. (2ND READER *takes book, exits.* SCARECROW *steps up to desk, sets book in front of* DOROTHY, *looks around furtively.* DOROTHY *pulls note out of book and reads it.*) "Dorothy, don't say a word. It's me." *(Looks up)* Scarecrow!

SCARECROW: Sh-h-h!

DOROTHY *(Grabbing his hand across table):* Scarecrow, what a surprise! I haven't heard from you in months!

SCARECROW *(Miserably):* Oh, Dorothy, everything's been terrible ever since we took that trip to the Emerald City!

DOROTHY: Why? You were so happy. The Wizard gave you a brain, just what you always wanted.

SCARECROW *(Shrugging):* I thought it's what I always wanted . . . until I found out how much work it is. Day in, day out, it's think, think, think.

3RD READER *(Pushing forward):* Hey—what's holding up the line?

DOROTHY: Scarecrow, I'd love to talk more, but as you can see you've caught me at a busy time.

SCARECROW: I should have thought of that.

DOROTHY: Why don't you stick around, and we can talk it over at lunch?

SCARECROW: Oh, Dorothy, that would be wonderful! I'll just read while I'm waiting.

DOROTHY: Good idea. (SCARECROW *crosses to browse at book shelves and gradually moves off right.* 3RD READER *steps up to desk, places stack of books in front of* DOROTHY, *then pulls list out of pocket and begins to read off names.*)

3RD READER *(Picking up book from pile):* Now, please make this one out to my cousin Eugene in Portland . . . and this one's to my sister Harriet in Harrisburg. And could you sign this one with happy birthday wishes to my nephew Elbert in Evanston, and—

TIN WOODMAN *(Stepping up behind* 3RD READER; *impatiently):* Can we get this line moving?

3RD READER *(Irritated):* Honestly, some people are so pushy!

DOROTHY: Why don't you just leave your list with me and come back for your books a little later this afternoon? I'll have them all ready for you.

3RD READER *(Fawning):* Miss Osbourne, you're such a dear. *(Hands her list and starts off)* Now, don't forget little Ophelia in Oshkosh and my brother Mortimer in Montpelier. *(Exits.* TIN WOODMAN *approaches desk.)*

TIN WOODMAN *(Dejectedly):* Hi, Dorothy!

DOROTHY *(Warmly):* Tin Woodman, I'm so glad to see you! Where did you come from?

TIN WOODMAN: I caught the first bus from Oz this morning.

DOROTHY: How *are* you?

TIN WOODMAN *(Sighing):* Dorothy, I just can't stand it any more.

DOROTHY: Why, what's wrong? The last time you wrote you had a wonderful job with the newspaper.

TIN WOODMAN: Yes, I wrote the advice-to-the-lovelorn column. People were always pouring out their hearts and seeking my advice.

DOROTHY: You should feel honored.

TIN WOODMAN: What I feel is depressed. I had no idea there was so much sadness in the world. If I had known that, I never would have asked the Wizard for a heart in the first place! *(Sobs)*

DOROTHY: There, there, don't cry. You'll rust your face.

4TH READER *(Stepping forward; irritated):* If you don't mind, I'd like to get home some time in this century.

TIN WOODMAN *(Drying his eyes):* Dorothy, are you free for lunch?

DOROTHY: Actually—

TIN WOODMAN *(Happily):* I knew you'd come through for me! I'll just go read until you're ready. *(Exits left)*

4TH READER *(Stepping up to desk):* Miss Osbourne, if you don't mind my advice—*(Places book in front of her)*

DOROTHY *(Smiling):* I'm always receptive to constructive criticism.

4TH READER: Good, because I think your writing needs more gusto, more pizzazz, if you know what I mean.

DOROTHY: No, I'm afraid I don't. *(Signs book)*

4TH READER: What I'm saying, Miss Osbourne, is that it's too cute, too much of a fairy tale. If you want to get anywhere as a writer, you're going to need more blood-and-guts realism, internal conflict, and—*(Loud roar is heard, as* DOROTHY *hands* 4TH READER *signed book.)* What was that? *(Moves to exit)*

DOROTHY: The roar of an impatient crowd, I'm afraid. (4TH READER *exits.* LION *enters and crosses to desk)*

LION: Oh, Dorothy, am I glad to see you!

DOROTHY *(Excitedly):* Lion! Look at you—all decked out in medals and ribbons. You're quite a sight.

LION: I'm also a nervous wreck.

DOROTHY: What's the trouble?

LION: I don't think I like being a hero, Dorothy. The pressure is too much. Ever since the Wizard gave me courage, I haven't had a moment's rest from protecting the kingdom.

DOROTHY *(Sympathetically)*: You poor thing.

LION *(Sighing)*: That's why I ran away. After all those stories you told me about how nothing ever happens in Kansas, I just knew this was the right place for me. (MS. FRITZ *appears in doorway.*)

MS. FRITZ: Lunchtime, Miss Osbourne. We'll see you back here in a half hour. *(She withdraws)*

LION: My timing is perfect—we can go to lunch and you can help me look through the classifieds for a nice, quiet job. (TIN WOODMAN *enters left, carrying book.*)

SCARECROW *(Entering from right)*: Well, Dorothy, are you ready—*(Abruptly)* What's going on? Tin Woodman? Lion? What are you doing here?

TIN WOODMAN *(Loftily)*: I have a perfectly logical excuse. I came to check out a book. *(Holds out book)*

LION *(To SCARECROW)*: And what are you doing here, Scarecrow?

SCARECROW: Me? Er—uh—give me a minute, the answer's on the tip of my tongue.

DOROTHY: Wait, all of you! Why don't you just admit the truth? Admit that you're not happy.

LION: Dorothy's absolutely right.

TIN WOODMAN: What do we do about it?

DOROTHY *(Shaking her head):* I wish I knew that myself.

SCARECROW: Of all of us, Dorothy, you seem the most content. A successful author, no less.

DOROTHY *(Sighing deeply):* Content? How can that be when I'm never home any more? Ever since I wrote this novel, I've been on the road, autographing books and speaking at colleges. Auntie Em is getting worn to a frazzle doing all the chores herself.

TIN WOODMAN: Maybe we never should have gone to Oz in the first place.

LION: We were probably better off the way we were.

SCARECROW: Then as I see it, there's only one solution.

OTHERS *(Together):* What?

SCARECROW: We've got to go back to Oz.

OTHERS *(Ad lib):* Back to Oz? Why? How can we? *(Etc.)*

SCARECROW: Why not? Surely the Wizard meets hundreds of people every day who think they want the same things that have made us miserable. It's only fair that we give them back.

LION *(Uncertainly):* I don't know. I didn't like going the first time. It was pretty scary. (LETITIA SHARPE *enters on last line. She looks like a witch.*)

LETITIA *(With evil laugh):* Scary, my pretties?

SCARECROW *(Frightened):* It's the witch, the Wicked Witch!

LION: She's back! The Wicked Witch!

DOROTHY *(Bravely):* No, it isn't. Though the resemblance is uncanny, it's really Letitia Sharpe, the schoolmarm of Topeka High. I'm sure she means us no harm.

LETITIA: A clever guess, but not clever enough.

TIN WOODMAN *(Fearfully):* What are you going to do?

LETITIA *(In a mean voice):* What I should have done a long time ago to this meddlesome girl and her stupid little dog! (DOROTHY *snatches up basket.)* Take all the credit and the fame, will you? Heh, heh, heh! A share of those royalties is mine, my pretty Dorothy.

ALL *(Amazed):* Yours?

LETITIA: Yes, mine! For maligning our family name and for dropping a house on my sister.

DOROTHY: It was all an accident, a mistake.

LION: It'll never happen again.

LETITIA: Heh, heh, heh. You can be sure of that, for with a wave of my hand, I'll—

PROFESSOR *(Over loudspeaker):* You'll what?

LETITIA *(Startled):* Who was that?

PROFESSOR *(Over loudspeaker):* You know perfectly well who I am, Letitia Sharpe. And you also know that it's impolite to harass people in libraries.

SCARECROW: That voice sounds familiar.

LION: It seems to be coming from behind that curtain. *(Timidly,* DOROTHY *approaches curtain and pulls it back.* PROFESSOR, *his back to audience, is speaking into a microphone.)*

PROFESSOR *(Into mike):* Pay no attention to that curtain.

DOROTHY: It's the Wizard!

PROFESSOR *(Turning):* What? Er—uh—yes, well, hello there. (DOROTHY, TIN WOODMAN, SCARE-CROW, *and* LION *rush up to* PROFESSOR, *who sets mike down.)*

TIN WOODMAN: Are we ever glad to see you!

LION: We're in a bit of trouble, Professor.

PROFESSOR: What seems to be the problem?

DOROTHY *(Pointing to* LETITIA): She claims that I owe her royalties on my latest book.

PROFESSOR *(Clearing his throat; pompously):* Yes, well, of course there are intricacies and legalities and ex post factos all to be considered, I suppose.

DOROTHY *(Worried):* That sounds complicated.

SCARECROW: Not really, Dorothy. All it means is that it could take forever clearing this up in court.

PROFESSOR: I think we could work out an equitable agreement—out of court. What do you say?

DOROTHY: It depends on what she wants.

PROFESSOR: And if it's fair, then will you give her a share?

DOROTHY *(Reluctantly):* I suppose so.

PROFESSOR *(To* LETITIA): Well then? What would you like? (LETITIA *approaches* DOROTHY, *walks around her, looks her up and down. She suddenly stops and points to* DOROTHY'S *shoes.*)

LETITIA: I want those!

TIN WOODMAN: Her feet?

LETITIA: Her shoes, you overgrown tin can. I want those ruby red slippers.

DOROTHY *(Protesting):* But Glinda told me not to take them off!

PROFESSOR: Not really, Dorothy. If you'll recall the conversation, Glinda told you not to take them off until you were safely back in Kansas. Which, of course, you are.

DOROTHY: This is true.

LETITIA: So do I get them or not?

PROFESSOR: Are you absolutely sure you want them?

LETITIA *(Angrily):* Of course I want them.

PROFESSOR: And you're most certain you won't change your mind?

LETITIA: I want the ruby red slippers, at once!

PROFESSOR: Give her the slippers, Dorothy.

DOROTHY: But—

PROFESSOR *(Firmly):* Just do as I say. (DOROTHY *takes off shoes and hands them to* LETITIA, *who eagerly tries to put them on.*)

LETITIA: Oo-hhh! Ouch!

PROFESSOR *(Mildly):* Is something wrong?

LETITIA *(Angrily):* These slippers are much too small. Ouch! Oo-oh!

SCARECROW: Why don't you take them off?

PROFESSOR: I'm afraid that's impossible, Scarecrow.

You see, we made a bargain. Letitia said she wanted the slippers more than anything else . . . *(Smiles)* and now she has them forever. (LETITIA, *howling, hops offstage. Others laugh.*)

DOROTHY *(Happily):* How can we thank you, Professor? You came just in the nick of time!

PROFESSOR: To be honest with you, my friends, I've been behind that curtain for quite a while . . . long enough to hear how unhappy you all were with the gifts I gave you.

SCARECROW: It's true, sir. Ever since you gave me a brain, people have come from far and wide to have me do their thinking for them.

TIN WOODMAN: And those with broken hearts have brought them to me for mending.

LION: And I'm tired of being courageous every second of the day.

PROFESSOR: What about you, Dorothy? Are you also dissatisfied with what you received—the knowledge that there's truly no place like home?

DOROTHY *(Sighing):* I think I knew that all along, Professor. The problem is that, once I put my adventures down on paper, I was too busy to enjoy my home.

SCARECROW: How about it, Professor? Can you put things back the way they were?

PROFESSOR *(Shaking his head):* Sadly, my friend, there is no returning to the past. A valuable lesson for each of you—you must be careful what you wish for, for it may come true.

DOROTHY *(Upset):* But there must be something you can do!

PROFESSOR *(Thinking a moment):* All I can offer is some simple advice.

SCARECROW: Please let us hear it.

PROFESSOR: For you, Scarecrow, enjoy being held in esteem, but be careful not to do your friends' thinking for them. Let them have the fun of finding answers on their own. They—and you—will be much happier.

TIN WOODMAN: How about me?

PROFESSOR: Ah, my sentimental friend. Too often of late you've seen the disadvantages of having such a fragile treasure as a heart, and in your generosity, you've sought to protect other hearts from breaking in two. Such actions, though, help you grow.

TIN WOODMAN: I just don't like seeing people get hurt.

PROFESSOR: True, true. Love can be painful. For sometimes those who fall head over heels in love don't always land on their feet. *(Pauses)* You must use your talent to help them pick themselves up. For it is time—and not magic—that heals all wounds.

LION: How about me? Life was simpler when I only had to be afraid of my shadow.

PROFESSOR: What an odd thing courage is, for one must constantly prove he has it! The problem, though, is that your strength has made others feel weak, for they have relied on you rather than on themselves.

DOROTHY: They should learn to say no.

PROFESSOR: As should you, my literary friend. *(Indicating books)* Writing a popular book is well and good, of course, but are you willing to pay the price for the time spent away from loved ones? (MS. FRITZ *enters.*)

MS. FRITZ: Oh, Miss Osbourne—back from lunch already? You're just in time, because we're expecting more of your fans any second.

DOROTHY: Excuse me, Ms. Fritz, but I was just about to leave for a reunion lunch with my friends.

MS. FRITZ: But our schedule—

DOROTHY *(Interrupting):* The schedule will have to be rearranged, I'm afraid. *(Links arms with her friends; happily)* Some things are just more important. (DOROTHY, SCARECROW, TIN WOODMAN, *and* LION *rush off.*)

MS. FRITZ *(Shaking her head):* These temperamental writers—I'll just never understand them. *(Notices* PROFESSOR) And who are you?

PROFESSOR: An old friend of the departing quartet. You'll join us, of course? *(Offering his arm)*

MS. FRITZ *(Smoothing her hair):* Why, yes, I'd love to, sir. *(Coyly)* I didn't have any plans at all . . . except to look at my travel magazines. I'm due for a vacation, you know.

PROFESSOR: Oh, really? Where were you planning to go?

MS. FRITZ: To be quite honest, I hadn't decided.
PROFESSOR *(Opening door for her):* If I could make
a recommendation—Emerald City is lovely this
time of year. *(They exit. Quick curtain)*

THE END

PRODUCTION NOTES

LESSONS OF OZ

Characters: 4 male; 3 female; 4 male or female for Readers.
Playing Time: 20 minutes.
Costumes: Dorothy, Scarecrow, Tin Woodman, Lion, and Professor
wear clothing similar to that of their movie counterparts. Dorothy
wears red shoes. Ms. Fritz wears skirt and sweater. Letitia Sharpe
is dressed like a schoolmarm and is made up like a witch. Readers
wear everyday clothes.
Properties: Several books; pen; basket; microphone.
Setting: The Topeka, Kansas, Public Library. Desk and chair are
down left. An easel with poster of book that reads KANSAS NEVER
LOOKED SO GOOD, BY DOROTHY OSBOURNE, is at right. Curtain
hangs behind desk. Table piled with books is next to working door,
up center. Backdrop shows stacks of books.
Lighting: No special effects.
Sound: Recorded music of "Over the Rainbow" may be played at
opening and closing, if desired.

Gopher Junction

Characters

JOE WALLACE, *Gopher Junction's sheriff*
SAGALONG DONOVAN, *his deputy*
MISS PURITY GOODY, *an elegantly dressed,
    mysterious lady*
DUSTY, *stagecoach driver*
DOC ⎫
LEN ⎪ *members of the Scagway Gang*
FRANK ⎬
CLYDE ⎭

SCENE 1

TIME: *Spring morning in the Old West.*
SETTING: *Main Street of Gopher Junction. In the
    foreground at left is sheriff's office; at right is two-
    story building with a veranda and double doors,
    above which hangs a sign reading,* GOPHER JUNC-

TION HOTEL. *Upstage is rustic saloon, with swinging doors. Next to it stands a white building with blue trim and curtains. Sign on front reads,* NELLY'S NITERY.

AT RISE: JOE WALLACE *enters from his office, closes door behind him, and looks up and down the street. He walks to center and addresses audience.*

JOE: This . . . is the city. Well, it isn't exactly a city. It's a little hick town, Gopher Junction, Crossroads of the West. To the east *(Indicating direction)* lies the Big City. North and south is Indian Territory. And to the west is That-a-Way, and That-a-Way's where most of the folks passing through are headed. *(Pauses)* This is a tough town. A man puts his life in the gun he wears. *(Whacks holster)* My name's Joe Wallace. I work here. I carry a badge. *(Walks back to office, then continues talking)* It was Tuesday, April 4th. We were working out of Burglary Division. My partner, Sagalong Donovan, was with me. (SAGALONG *enters from office and looks at pocketwatch.*)

SAGALONG: Hey, Joe, it's almost 10:15—time for the stage to be gettin' in.

JOE *(Smiling):* Thanks for reminding me, Sagalong. I'd better mosey over to meet it; somebody may try to rob it. Want to tag along, Sagalong? *(Starts right)*

SAGALONG *(Happily):* Whatever you say, Joe. *(Joins him)* I have to hand it to you, Joe. Since you came here from the Big City, we've had real law and order in this town. You have a fantastic system. *(They pause, right.)*

JOE: That's right. Bunco Squad on Monday, Burglary on Tuesday, Homicide on Thursday . . .

SAGALONG: You left out Wednesday, Joe.

JOE: That's the day I go to Rotary luncheons.

SAGALONG: It's still a great system.

JOE: Ah-h-h—I don't want to take all the credit for it, Sagalong. It's the same way we did things in Tucumcari when I was a deputy. *(Sound of horses' hooves is heard offstage.* SAGALONG *looks off right, whistles and nudges* JOE.*)*

SAGALONG: Wow, Joe—look at that girl gettin' off the stage. Pretty, huh? *(Continues to stare)*

JOE *(Fumbling in pocket):* Wait till I get out my glasses. *(Puts on a pair of wireframes and squints)*

SAGALONG: Zow-ee! I wonder if she's one of the new girls for the saloon.

JOE *(Annoyed):* Can't you tell a lady when you see one? Hm-m-m . . . she looks like a society lady from the East. I'll have to greet her properly. *(Puts glasses back in pocket.* PURITY GOODY *enters, looking around; she carries a large satchel under her arm.* JOE *strides up to her, takes off his hat, and clears his throat.)* Howdy, ma'am. Welcome to Gopher Junction. *(Smiles; shyly)* I'm Joe Wallace, Sheriff in these parts and known as the fastest left-handed gun in the West!

PURITY *(Startled):* The sheriff! Oh, my!

JOE: Yes, ma'am. I could tell just by looking at you that you're a society lady from the East! (PURITY *smiles and extends a hand.*)

PURITY *(In Southern drawl):* Why, I just happen to be from the eastern part of the South! What a perceptive man you are!

JOE *(Embarrassed):* Yes, well, uh . . . say, I don't believe I caught *your* name, ma'am.

PURITY: I don't believe I dropped it, Sheriff. It's Miss Purity Goody.

JOE: Pleasure's mine, ma'am. *(To* SAGALONG, *who stands, staring at* PURITY) Don't just stand there, Sagalong—get Miss Purity's bags for her.

PURITY *(Quickly):* Please, don't bother. *(Indicates satchel)* I have just the one.

SAGALONG *(Reaching for it):* Allow me!

PURITY *(Pulling it away; sharply):* No, thank you. I can manage. *(Sweetly)* I really can.

JOE *(To* SAGALONG): You heard the lady, Sagalong. Why don't you go dust the jail or something? (*As* SAGALONG *starts to go,* JOE *addresses* PURITY.) Like to keep things neat, you know.

PURITY: That's very commendable, Sheriff. (SAGALONG *exits.*)

JOE: Just the one bag, ma'am?

PURITY: Yes, I'll be staying here only a short time. I'm meeting someone. By the way, would you happen to know a good hotel?

JOE *(Gesturing):* Finest hotel in Gopher Junction,

ma'am. *(Steps on to hotel veranda and opens the door)* I'm sure you'll find it just fine.

PURITY *(Shaking his hand again):* Why, how lucky can a girl be—meetin' a handsome man the minute she steps off the stage! I declare I'm going to like it here! *(Goes into hotel)*

SAGALONG *(Coming out of office; to* JOE*):* You sure have a way with women, Joe. (DUSTY, *carrying roll of paper, enters from right.)*

DUSTY: Hey, Sheriff! I have to talk to you!

JOE: Here I am, Dusty. What's up?

DUSTY *(Wiping forehead with kerchief):* The notorious Scagway Gang escaped from prison last week! Rumor has it they're headed this way!

JOE *(Alarmed):* The Scagway Gang? Why, no bank will be safe till they're apprehended. Do you have an M.O. on them?

DUSTY: Nope. But I've got some W.P.'s.

JOE: W.P.'s? What's that?

DUSTY: Wanted posters. *(Hands them to* JOE, *who pulls out glasses and studies posters)*

JOE: Hm-m-m. . . . They don't look like the criminal type.

DUSTY *(Pointing to poster):* All of 'em are there— except for their female accomplice.

SAGALONG: A female?

DUSTY: Yes, and if you find her, it shouldn't be too hard to catch the rest. Seems they entrusted her with all the loot from their last job. They'll have to get together to divvy it up.

JOE: Aha! *Cherchez la femme!*

DUSTY: What?

JOE: Never mind. That's French. (*Hands posters to* SAGALONG) Put these posters up right away, Sagalong. (*To* DUSTY) Good thing you brought 'em on a Tuesday—today's Burglary Division. Otherwise, this case would have to wait till next week. (SAGALONG *exits*.)

DUSTY: See you later, Joe! (*Exits.* JOE *goes into office. Curtain*)

* * * * *

SCENE 2

TIME: *Early evening*.

SETTING: *Same. The walls of the buildings are decked with wanted posters*.

AT RISE: *The sound of player piano music comes forth from the saloon.* JOE *and* SAGALONG *enter from office*.

SAGALONG (*Proudly*): I put up all the posters, Joe, but I hope that notorious Scagway Gang doesn't decide to come here.

JOE (*Confidentially*): If they do, we'll get 'em, Sagalong. By the way, did Miss Purity settle in at the hotel?

SAGALONG: Yes.

JOE: Hm-m-m . . . I wonder if she'd like to have dinner with me tonight?

SAGALONG: I don't know, Joe. She said she was

tired—she's having dinner sent up to her room. Speakin' of dinner, Joe, what do you say we try out that new place, Nelly's Nitery? It's run by Nelly Nickerson, Ned Nickerbocker's niece from Nebraska, who knits and collects knickknacks.

JOE: Sounds nice. *(They walk toward restaurant.)*

SAGALONG: You'll like this place, Joe. *(They exit into Nitery, as* PURITY *enters from hotel. She carries satchel. She sees posters, stops to look at them.)*

PURITY *(To herself):* My, oh, my! That picture surely doesn't do Clyde justice—he's far better looking than that! Though this one of Doc's not half-bad. *(As she says this,* DOC *enters from behind hotel.)*

DOC: No, it isn't, is it?

PURITY *(Gasping in surprise):* Why, Doc—what are you doing here?

DOC *(With a smirk):* Making a house call on my favorite partner-in-crime. *(Takes her hand and kisses it)*

PURITY: You can pour on all the charm you like, Doc, but your sweet-talk's not going to get you anywhere. You know the plan as well as I do! We wait here for Clyde and the others.

DOC: No time for that, Purity. They're closing in on us. There are wanted posters every place you turn!

PURITY: So?

DOC: So it's time you and I get out of here, Purity. If

we leave together, it'll avert suspicion. Get the money, and we'll leave on the next stage!

PURITY (*Firmly*): I'm not ready to go yet, Doc. I'm waiting for Clyde and the rest as planned.

DOC: But it's not safe for either one of us here!

PURITY (*Laughing*): Speak for yourself, Doc. My picture's not on any of those posters.

DOC: Be sensible, Purity. The loot will go a lot further if we divide it two ways instead of five!

PURITY (*Pulling away*): I'm not going, Doc.

DOC (*Spying satchel*): Is that the money? Give it to me! (*Grabs for bag; she pulls it back. They are struggling as* JOE *and* SAGALONG *enter from Nellie's Nitery.*)

JOE (*To* SAGALONG): I told you I can't read menus without my glasses! How could you let me forget them?

SAGALONG (*Seeing* PURITY *and* DOC): Hey, Joe— look! (PURITY *pulls gun out of satchel.* DOC *wrestles bag from her.*)

PURITY (*Aiming gun at* DOC): Drop the bag, Doc! (DOC *complies.* JOE *moves beside her.*)

JOE: Evening, Miss Purity. What's going on?

PURITY: This man tried to steal my satchel. I want him locked up immediately.

DOC (*Shocked*): What!

JOE (*Striding up to* DOC): We got rules about stealing satchels in this town, stranger. A couple nights in jail ought to teach you a lesson about accosting ladies.

DOC *(Protesting):* But, but—

JOE: Book him, Sagalong. (SAGALONG *escorts* DOC *into office.*)

PURITY *(Sobbing on* JOE's *shoulder):* Why, Sheriff, I just don't know what I would've done if you hadn't come along!

JOE *(Indicating gun):* Maybe I'd better take that for you, Miss Purity. Seems dangerous for a little lady like you to carry a gun.

PURITY *(Hesitating):* You're probably right, Sheriff. Why, I hardly know how to shoot it at all. *(Handing it to him)* You will take good care of it, won't you? It's the only thing of my daddy's I've got left. *(Sniffs)* I'd absolutely die if I ever lost it!

JOE *(Handing it back):* Well, on second thought, ma'am, I wouldn't want anything to happen to it while it's in my possession. Why don't you just go ahead and keep it?

PURITY *(Putting it back in satchel):* I'd better get back to my room now—I'm feelin' a bit shaken. *(Squeezes his hand, as she pauses at door of hotel)* Goodnight, Sheriff. *(Exits)*

SAGALONG *(Emerging from office):* I booked him, Joe, and guess what?

JOE: What?

SAGALONG: He's Doc Wishbone of the Scagway Gang! Right here in our very jail! Can you believe it?

JOE *(Worried):* I wonder if that means the rest of the gang is headed this way.

SAGALONG: One thing puzzles me, Joe.

JOE: What's that?

SAGALONG: I might be mistaken, but I think I heard Miss Purity call him by name just before we rescued her.

JOE *(Shrugging):* Probably recognized him from the posters.

SAGALONG *(Uncertainly):* That's probably it. *(Exits into office. JOE stands in front of DOC's poster, pulls it down and looks in direction of hotel as curtain closes.)*

* * * * *

SCENE 3

TIME: *The next morning.*

SETTING: *The same.*

AT RISE: PURITY *enters from hotel;* SHERIFF *enters from office. They meet center.*

JOE: Morning, Miss Purity.

PURITY: Morning, Sheriff.

JOE: Care to join me for a cup of coffee at Nelly's Nitery?

PURITY: No, thank you. I just thought I'd soak up some of your sunshine for a while. *(Puts hand on his arm)* You will give me a raincheck, though, won't you?

JOE: Of course! *(Tips hat)* If you need anything, Sagalong and I will be over at the Nitery for a while.

PURITY: I'll remember, Sheriff. (*He exits. A moment later,* LEN *and* FRANK *enter from behind hotel and come up on either side of* PURITY.)

LEN: Howdy, Purity.

FRANK: Howdy, Purity.

PURITY (*Puzzled; slowly):* Len? Frank? What are you doing here?

LEN: Stole a couple of horses and got here ahead of schedule.

PURITY: Why, I hardly recognized you boys at first!

FRANK: Good disguise, huh? Len dyed his hair, and I got this moustache. How do you like it? (*Twirls moustache)*

PURITY: It suits you, Frank. You two look downright respectable!

LEN: Hey, Purity! How come there's no picture of Doc up anywhere?

PURITY (*Sighing):* I heard he was arrested for trying to steal something.

FRANK (*With an evil laugh):* All the better—one less partner to split the loot with.

LEN: Four instead of five, right, Purity?

PURITY: Sounds right to me.

FRANK: Speaking of which . . .

PURITY: Yes?

LEN: Three is even better. How about it?

PURITY: What on earth are you boys talking about?

FRANK: We're talking about cutting Clyde out. Are you in?

PURITY: I'll have to think about it. Why don't you

boys just go find something to do for a little while, and I'll get back to you.

LEN: Hey, that's a good idea! What do you say we go scope out that bank, Frank?

FRANK: What for, Len?

LEN: To rob it, of course.

FRANK *(Nodding):* That's a good idea. Doesn't hurt to stay in practice. *(They start to exit.)*

PURITY: Oh, boys?

PURITY: Oh, boys? I found out something you might want to know, "bank-wise."

FRANK: What's that?

PURITY: They don't keep their money in the bank safe. They keep the vault over there—*(Points)* in Nelly's Nitery.

FRANK: How come?

PURITY: So no one can steal the money, of course.

LEN: That makes sense to me.

FRANK *(To* PURITY): Are you serious?

PURITY: Why, I hear the Nitery vault hasn't been robbed in fifty years!

LEN: Well, we're about to make history. Come on, Frank! *(Exits into Nitery)*

FRANK *(To* PURITY): Be right back, Purity. We'll handle this heist with our usual finesse. *(Exits into Nitery. After a moment, muffled shouts are heard.* SAGALONG *enters with* LEN *and* FRANK, *whom he escorts into office. In the meantime,* PURITY *hides around the corner so they can't see her.* JOE *enters from Nitery, puts his gun into his holster.* PURITY *steps out to greet him.)*

PURITY: Oh, Sheriff?

JOE *(Tipping his hat):* I'm in sort of a hurry, ma'am.

PURITY: What's going on? Who were those two men?

JOE: Strangest thing, Miss Purity. We were just drinking our coffee when those two characters burst in, looking for the bank vault. Can you believe it? Anyway, Sagalong recognized them from the posters.

PURITY *(Feigning alarm):* You can't mean—

JOE: Brace yourself, ma'am. They're members of the notorious Scagway Gang.

PURITY *(Pretending alarm):* Right here in town?

JOE: Everything's under control, though. Three down and two to go. *(Takes down posters with pictures of* LEN *and* FRANK*)*

PURITY: Two, Sheriff? There's only one picture left.

JOE: That's 'cause the last one is a woman, and we don't have a picture of her.

PURITY: I see.

JOE: I've never arrested a woman before. *(Shrugs)* Well, the law's the law.

PURITY: Yes, I suppose so.

JOE: I really do have to go now. *(Tips hat)* Talk to you later. *(Exits into office; curtain)*

* * * * *

SCENE 4

TIME: *Early evening.*

SETTING: *Same.*

AT RISE: JOE *and* SAGALONG *enter from office.*

SAGALONG: I still can't get over it, Joe—that fellow last night and the two this morning are all members of the notorious Scagway Gang. Do you think it means they were planning to meet here in Gopher Junction to divvy up the dough?

JOE: Looks that way, Sagalong. There's a big reward for their capture, you know, and I could use the money.

SAGALONG: Oh? You never complained about money before, Joe.

JOE: Well, I'm plannin' on makin' a few changes around here.

SAGALONG: What kind of changes, Joe?

JOE: Well, I've been thinkin' about takin' on a partner for life.

SAGALONG *(Upset):* Really, Joe—I always thought *we* were partners. You said you liked the way I handled that Forthwright case last week. And how about the time those rustlers were hiding horses in the hotel? And what about—

JOE: That's not what I meant, ol' pal. What I had in mind was a young lady.

SAGALONG *(Shaking his head):* Well, I don't know, Joe. I've never heard of any lady deputies. But you're the boss, Joe. If that's the way you feel—

JOE *(Laughing):* You knucklehead! I'm talking about getting married! *(Proudly)* To Miss Purity.

SAGALONG *(Brightening):* Gosh! Congratulations, Joe! That's terrific!

JOE: As a matter of fact, I think I'll ask her tonight.

I'll take her over to Nelly's for dinner and pop the question. *(As they talk,* CLYDE SCAGWAY *enters right. He sees poster and glances around nervously.)*

SAGALONG *(Indicating* CLYDE): Stranger comin', Joe.

JOE *(Waving to* CLYDE): Howdy, stranger!

CLYDE *(Composing himself):* Good evening, gentlemen.

SAGALONG: Evenin'.

CLYDE: Perhaps you could assist me. I'm looking for the hotel. I'm supposed to meet my fiancée there.

SAGALONG: Right over there.

CLYDE: Thank you. *(Enters hotel)*

JOE *(Scratching his head):* You know, Sagalong, there's something mighty familiar about that man.

SAGALONG: Yeah, Joe, I thought so too.

JOE: I just have the feeling I've seen him before.

SAGALONG: Me, too, Joe. Sharp dresser, wasn't he?

JOE: Uh-huh. Who do you suppose his fiancée is?

SAGALONG *(Shrugging):* There's only one woman I know of at the hotel. *(Hesitates)*

JOE *(Sighing):* Go ahead and say it, Sagalong.

SAGALONG: Miss Purity. *(Sympathetically)* I'm really sorry, Joe. 'Course, maybe it's not Miss Purity at all.

JOE: No, Sagalong, it stands to reason that a good-looking woman like Purity wouldn't stay unattached for long.

SAGALONG: Are you going to go over and find out?

JOE *(Shrugging):* What's the use? We both already know the answer. *(Walks into office,* SAGALONG *slowly following.* PURITY *and* CLYDE *enter from hotel;* PURITY *carries satchel.)*

PURITY *(Gushing):* I just can't tell you how tickled I am to see you, Clyde, dear.

CLYDE: Not as tickled as I'll be to see all that money!

PURITY *(Coyly):* Why, if I didn't know you better, Clyde, I'd think you came all this way just to see the money!

CLYDE: Nonsense! *(Takes her in his arms, as* JOE *enters from office; neither* CLYDE *nor* PURITY *sees him)*

PURITY *(Pushing him away):* Clyde, really! *(During following conversation,* JOE *listens quietly, scratching his head, as if perplexed. He suddenly turns to look at wanted poster, fumbles with glasses, puts them on, looks closely at poster, then at* CLYDE.)*

CLYDE: Where are the others?

PURITY *(Smoothly):* Slight change of plan, Clyde.

CLYDE *(Suspiciously):* How slight?

PURITY: Well, Doc was arrested for trying to steal the satchel, and Len and Frank were arrested for trying to rob the cafe.

CLYDE: Why did they do that?

PURITY: They were confused. They thought the cafe was the bank.

CLYDE: Those dumb clucks!

PURITY: So it's just the two of us, now, Clyde.

CLYDE: Yes, it is, isn't it? (JOE, *hand on holster, moves toward* CLYDE.)

JOE: Hold it right there, Clyde Scagway! This is the end of the line for you.

CLYDE *(Turning):* I beg your pardon?

JOE: I know who you are—you're Clyde Scagway!

CLYDE *(To* PURITY): This will take just a minute.

JOE: I'm warning you, Clyde. I'm the fastest left-handed gun in the West.

CLYDE: I'm the fastest right-handed gun.

JOE: Oh.

PURITY *(Pulling gun out of satchel):* Oh, Clyde?

CLYDE: In a minute, Purity. (PURITY *cocks gun, aims at* CLYDE, *who wheels around.*) What's going on?

PURITY: As he said, Clyde, it's the end of the line for you. (JOE *takes out his own gun, aims it at* CLYDE, *who raises his arms over his head.*)

SAGALONG *(Bursting out of office):* Hey, Joe, I just figured out who—(*Sees* CLYDE) Oh, I see you already figured it out for yourself.

JOE: Book him, Sagalong. (SAGALONG *pulls out gun and escorts* CLYDE *to office.* JOE *puts his gun into holster.*)

CLYDE *(Angrily; to* PURITY): You haven't heard the last of me, Purity. (*Exits into office with* SAGALONG)

PURITY *(Twirling gun and putting it back into sat-*

chel): Well, Sheriff, all four members of the Scag-way Gang are now in your very own jail.

JOE *(Sadly):* Not quite, Miss Purity.

PURITY: No?

JOE: There were five of them. The fifth was a woman. *(Sighs)* And I think I know who she is.

PURITY: Are you going to arrest me, Joe?

JOE *(Shaking his head):* I can't, ma'am. *(Indicating satchel)* I assume the money is in that satchel?

PURITY: All of it, Sheriff. *(Starts to hand it to him)*

JOE *(Refusing):* Take it and get out of town.

PURITY: I don't understand.

JOE: I can't arrest you, Miss Purity. I love you. I was going to ask you to be my wife. *(Nobly)* I'll turn in my badge tomorrow.

PURITY *(Smiling):* That won't be necessary, Joe. *(Reaches into satchel)* Because I'll turn in mine! *(Holds out shiny star)*

JOE *(Puzzled):* What do you mean?

PURITY: My real name is Elizabeth Branch. I'm a special investigator for Wells Fargo.

JOE: But I thought—

PURITY: That I was a member of the gang? *(Laughs)* It took a lot of work, but I managed to get the gang's confidence and make them think I was as greedy as they were.

JOE: How did you do that?

PURITY: A few years as an actress on the New York stage helped. I gave a convincing performance as a society girl in search of adventure and excitement and talked them into letting me hold the money for safekeeping until we were able to meet somewhere and divide it.

JOE: Why Gopher Junction?

PURITY *(In official tone):* Your reputation as a defender of law and justice is well known, Sheriff. I knew that they'd be hard to handle on my own, so I suggested we meet here, knowing you'd help me wrap up the Scagway case once and for all. *(Linking her arm through his)* It's nice to know I'm ending my career on such a positive note!

JOE: Ending your career?

PURITY: I believe you mentioned something about marriage?

JOE *(Overjoyed):* Do you mean—you'll marry me?

SAGALONG *(Entering):* They're all taken care of, Joe . . . all except for the woman.

JOE: And I intend to do just that—take good care of her forever.

SAGALONG: But isn't she—

JOE: She's one of us, Sagalong. And she just said yes!

SAGALONG: Hey, congratulations! (*Sighs; to* PURITY) And to think we almost arrested you as a member of the notorious Scagway Gang!

PURITY (*To* JOE): Are you going to give me a life sentence, Joe?

JOE *(Smiling):* You can count on it! *(Curtain)*

THE END

PRODUCTION NOTES

GOPHER JUNCTION

Characters: 1 female; 7 male.

Playing Time: 20 minutes.

Costumes: Nineteenth-century western clothing for all. Purity is dressed elegantly. Joe and Sagalong wear toy holsters and guns, silver stars. Sagalong has pocketwatch; Joe has wire-rim glasses in pocket.

Properties: Satchel with toy gun and silver star in it; wanted posters.

Setting: Main Street of Gopher Junction. In the foreground at left is sheriff's office; at right is two-story building with a veranda and double doors, above which hangs a sign reading, GOPHER JUNCTION HOTEL. Upstage is rustic saloon, with swinging doors. Next to it stands a white building with blue trim and curtains. Sign on front read's NELLY'S NITERY.

Lighting: No special effects.

Sound: Horses' hooves; player piano music.

Shadow of Dracula

Characters

ERIC RATHSKELLER
MILO RATHSKELLER
BARBARA CARSON
MURIEL CARSON, *her mother*

TIME: *The present; an autumn evening.*

SETTING: *Estate of the late Count Siegfried von Rathskeller—a Gothic mansion steeped in Old-World tradition. Fireplace is up right. A skull sits on the mantel. Table with wine glasses on it stands right, and two chairs, left. Floor-to-ceiling bookcases provide backdrop.*

AT RISE: *Standing in front of fireplace, ERIC nervously checks his wristwatch, adjusts his tie, and quickly smooths his hair. As he does so, MILO, in floor-length black cape, silently appears from behind wall up left.*

ERIC (*Starting to cross stage left, then noticing* MILO): Well! It's about time!

MILO (*Retorting with annoyance*): Spare the sarcasm—the sun's been down only five minutes.

ERIC (*Looking at watch*): For your information—

MILO (*Interrupting him*): All right—ten at the most.

ERIC: I've been looking all over for you.

MILO (*Running his fingers over the back of chair, then holding out his hand*): Did you dust?

ERIC: Of *course* I did. Why?

MILO: How am I supposed to leave you notes if there's no dust?

ERIC: I'll buy you some paper.

MILO (*Surveying room critically*): I suppose you got rid of the shrouds, too?

ERIC (*Puzzled*): You mean all the sheets you had over the furniture?

MILO (*With air of superiority*): You call them sheets; I call them shrouds. (*Looks around*) Where are they?

ERIC (*Crossing to downstage window*): I put them upstairs.

MILO (*Following him*): But the furniture's down here.

ERIC (*Turning to explain*): We're having guests, remember?

MILO: So?

ERIC (*Impatiently*): So I can't have them walking

into a room decorated in . . . *(Searches for the right words)* Early Nightmare.

MILO *(Shrugging):* It looked fine to me.

ERIC: That's because you're used to it.

MILO *(Miffed):* I'm also used to being told what's going on.

ERIC: I told you three weeks ago.

MILO: You told me you'd think it over.

ERIC: Well, I did.

MILO: And?

ERIC: And I haven't changed my mind. I love Barbara, and she's going to be my wife.

MILO *(Smugly):* If you ask me, you're making a big mistake.

ERIC: I'm not asking you.

MILO: Only because you don't want me to say, "I told you so."

ERIC *(Turning to face him):* Will you try to understand? This evening is very important to me. All I'm asking is that you stay out of the house for a few hours.

MILO *(Shrewdly):* You didn't tell her yet, did you?

ERIC: I *was* going to tell her tonight.

MILO *(Satisfied):* Fine. Then you can introduce me. It'll be just like show-and-tell.

ERIC *(Correcting him):* I said *was*. Past tense.

MILO: What do you mean—was?

ERIC: I can't tell her tonight.

MILO: Why not?

ERIC *(Hesitating):* She's . . . bringing someone.

MILO: Who? The Exorcist?

ERIC: Her mother.

MILO *(Annoyed):* She's not going to live here *too*, is she?

ERIC: No, she just wants to see the house.

MILO: Is she staying for dinner?

ERIC: Yes.

MILO *(Hurt):* Why is it that she gets to stay and I don't?

ERIC *(Patiently):* Because she's Barbara's mother.

MILO: So what am I? A chair? You wouldn't even have a house to take her to if it weren't for me.

ERIC *(Relenting):* All right. Would you like to have dinner with us?

MILO *(Noncommittally):* I don't know. *(Strolls to fireplace)* What are we having?

ERIC: Steaks.

MILO *(Annoyed, with hands on hips):* You said that just to upset me. You know how much I hate steaks.

ERIC *(Shrugging):* Suit yourself.

MILO *(After a moment):* Well, I guess I'll stay if you really want me to.

ERIC: You can stay if you behave yourself . . . and change your clothes.

MILO *(Vexed):* So now my *clothes* embarrass you? *(Looks down at himself)* What's wrong with my clothes?

ERIC: I can't have you walking around here like an

extra from some Shakespearean tragedy (MILO *removes the skull from mantel.*)—not with Barbara and her mother here.

MILO *(In English accent):* I fail to see the humor of that remark, sir. "But let your own discretion be your tutor, suit the action to the word, the word to the action; with this special observance, that you o'erstep not the modesty of nature . . ."

ERIC *(With arms folded):* Are you finished?

MILO *(Pleased):* Would you like to hear more?

ERIC: What I'd like to hear is the sound of your footsteps going back downstairs, where you belong.

MILO *(Returning skull to mantel, sulkily):* Well, I certainly know when I've been slighted.

ERIC *(Annoyed):* Do you really?

MILO: What do you mean?

ERIC: Have you taken a good look at yourself lately?

MILO: Lately? No.

ERIC: Do you know what you'd see?

MILO *(Shrugging):* Probably nothing.

ERIC: Well, I'll tell you what you'd see. *(With his back to MILO, who pantomimes the emotions ERIC lists)* Someone who's conceited . . . and greedy . . . and selfish . . . and so . . . so wrapped up in himself that—*(He turns to look at MILO, who has wrapped his cape around his head. ERIC stops talking, and after a moment, MILO unwraps himself.)*

MILO *(Sheepishly):* It was so quiet in here, I

thought you'd left.

ERIC *(With eyes upward):* Why me?

MILO *(Crossing to* ERIC *and throwing an arm around his shoulder):* Look at the bright side.

ERIC: There isn't one.

MILO: Yes, there is. Listen. I have my own room, keep strict hours—you won't even know that I'm around.

ERIC: How will I explain the coffin in the cellar? Barbara's bound to notice it.

MILO *(Pacing back and forth, then suddenly snapping his fingers):* I know! We'll put green felt on top of the coffin and tell her it's a pool table.

ERIC *(Sarcastically):* Oh, sure.

MILO: You don't even have to find friends for me.

ERIC: I've *met* some of your friends, Milo.

MILO: And?

ERIC: Don't bring them home.

MILO: It's my home just as much as yours. *(Smugly)* Unless you want to contest the will in court.

ERIC *(Crossing to window):* I have it on good authority that the court meets in broad daylight.

MILO: Oh, I hadn't thought of that.

ERIC *(Anxiously):* Listen, a car just pulled up. *(Pleading)* For once, Milo, will you—

MILO: I'll be myself.

ERIC: That's what I'm afraid of.

MILO: Anything else?

ERIC: Would you please change your clothes?

MILO: I'll put on a tie.

ERIC *(Turning to exit):* Oh, Milo. Sometimes you're a real cross to bear. *(Exits)*

MILO *(Scowling):* Drat! First he gets rid of the dust . . . then he gets rid of the shrouds. Next thing you know, he'll probably want to get rid of *me*. *(Shaking his head as he paces)* If Grandfather von Rathskeller knew what was happening, he'd roll over in his grave. *(Musing)* He probably *is* rolling over in his grave. *(Suddenly)* As long as he's up, I think I'll go ask him. (*Quickly exits up right, as* ERIC *re-enters with* BARBARA CARSON *and* MURIEL CARSON.)

MURIEL *(Impressed; in loud stage whisper):* You didn't tell me he was rich, Barbara.

ERIC *(Laughing):* Don't let the facade fool you, Mrs. Carson. *(Looking around)* My ancestors spent enough to leave the next five generations in debt.

MURIEL *(Taking* BARBARA *aside; concerned):* Maybe you should reconsider this, dear.

BARBARA (*Reassuring her mother and crossing to* ERIC): Nonsense! Eric and I both work—we'll manage just fine.

MURIEL: Then who's going to take care of the children? *(Crosses to window, looks out)*

ERIC *(To* BARBARA; *nervously):* What children?

BARBARA: I forgot to warn you—Mother's chief ambition is to have grandchildren to dote on.

ERIC: Wouldn't it be cheaper to buy her a dog?

MURIEL *(At window):* I didn't notice *that* when we drove up.

BARBARA *(Joining her):* What?

MURIEL *(Pointing):* That decorative little garden.

ERIC *(Awkwardly):* Actually, it's not . . .

MURIEL: Too many flowers, though—it almost looks like a cemetery.

ERIC: That's because it is one.

MURIEL *(Shocked):* What? A cemetery in your backyard!

ERIC: It's been there since the early 1800's.

MURIEL *(Shuddering):* Awfully creepy, if you ask me.

ERIC *(Shrugging):* We don't bother the spirits, so they don't bother us.

MURIEL *(Unconvinced):* I don't see why you couldn't have stayed downtown.

BARBARA *(To* MURIEL): But this is Eric's homestead, Mother. He inherited it. (MILO *enters up right; he is wearing a red bow tie. He surveys group and leans his elbow on mantel.)* Eric is the last of the Rathskellers.

MURIEL: What happened to the rest of them?

BARBARA *(Annoyed):* Mother, really! (ERIC *notices* MILO *and quickly slips to his side, pantomiming that he wants him to leave and change his clothes.)*

MURIEL: You can't be too careful. Families like that, Barbara *(Shaking her head)*—you never know *what* kind of skeletons they have in their closets!

BARBARA *(Reassuring her):* I'm sure if there were any secrets, Eric wouldn't hesitate to tell me.

(Turning) Isn't that right—(BARBARA *and* MURIEL *see* ERIC *and* MILO. MILO *smiles and points at women;* ERIC *turns around, laughs nervously.)* Eric?

ERIC *(Stepping in front of* MILO *deliberately):* Yes? (MILO *waves behind him.)*

BARBARA: Aren't you going to introduce us?

ERIC: Uh—well—

MILO *(Tapping* ERIC *on shoulder):* If you don't introduce me, I'm going to flap my arms and fly around the room. Try to explain *that* one.

ERIC *(Reaching out to* BARBARA, *who walks over and takes his hand):* Uh, Barbara—*(Quickly)* This is my fiancée, Barbara.

MILO *(With an assumed accent):* Good evening. *(Kisses her hand)*

ERIC (*Quickly taking* MILO's *arm and escorting him over to* MURIEL): And this is Barbara's mother, Mrs. Carson.

MURIEL *(Extending her hand to be kissed):* Call me Muriel.

MILO: Good evening, Madam. *(He kisses her hand, then proceeds to plant kisses all the way up her arm.)*

BARBARA: Eric, haven't you forgotten something?

ERIC *(Nervously):* What?

BARBARA: You've introduced us . . . but not your friend.

ERIC *(Laughing nervously):* I didn't? *(Turns and sees that* MILO *has reached* MURIEL's *neck.* ERIC *lunges forward and pulls* MILO *away.)* Uh, this is—*(Thinking quickly)* my brother, Milo.

MILO: *Count* Milo.

MURIEL *(Impressed):* I didn't know your brother was a count, Eric.

BARBARA *(To* ERIC): I didn't even know you had a brother.

MILO *(To* MURIEL): I'm pleased to say that royalty runs through my veins. *(Casually)* As a matter of fact, just the other night—

ERIC *(Interrupting):* Milo, why don't you get us some wine from the cellar?

MILO *(Annoyed):* You could have saved me a trip . . .

ERIC *(With teeth clenched):* Just *do* it. *(Smiling weakly)* Please. (MILO *flings one end of his cape over his shoulder and exits dramatically.)* Where were we?

MURIEL: We were talking about your brother—he's such a *courtly* young man. Didn't you think so, Barbara?

BARBARA *(Uneasily):* Yes—and such unusual clothes, too.

MURIEL *(Thinking):* He reminds me of someone.

ERIC: He does?

MURIEL: Hamlet, I think. Doesn't he remind you of Hamlet, Barbara?

MILO *(Offstage; dramatically):* "To be or not to be . . . *(Enters, carrying black bottle and huge spray of flowers)* that is the question."

ERIC *(Sarcastically):* What took you so long?

BARBARA *(Impressed with his speed):* You must have *flown* down the stairs!

MILO *(Shaking his finger at her):* Tsk. Tsk. Tsk. No fair peeking.

MURIEL: What lovely flowers!

MILO *(Crossing to her):* For you.

MURIEL *(Coyly):* You shouldn't have.

MILO *(Casually):* I picked them on my way.

ERIC *(In realization):* You *didn't!*

BARBARA *(Puzzled):* Didn't what?

MURIEL *(Reading tag on flowers):* Who's Gideon Nelson?

MILO: You didn't know Gideon? Why, he's—

ERIC *(Quickly):* The florist. *(To* BARBARA*)* Gideon Nelson, the florist. Isn't that right, Milo?

MILO: Actually—

MURIEL *(Reading tag):* R.I.P.?

ERIC *(Quickly):* "Roses in person." *(To* BARBARA*)* That's his motto.

MILO *(Pleasantly):* He would have come himself, but—

ERIC *(Bursting in on conversation):* How about some wine? *(Gets glasses)*

MILO *(Holding up bottle):* A splendid idea!

BARBARA: What an unusual bottle, Milo. *(Taking glass from* ERIC*)*

MILO *(Proudly):* My private stock—for *special* occasions. *(Starts to pour wine—which is very thick and bright red—into* BARBARA's *glass)*

BARBARA: It's awfully thick, isn't it?

ERIC *(Puzzled):* I don't remember seeing that kind before.

MURIEL *(Helpfully):* Maybe it's not chilled properly.

MILO (*Handing a glass to* BARBARA): On the contrary . . . *(With knowing smile)* It's best served at 98.6 degrees Fahrenheit.

ERIC (*Realizing what it is; trying to grab glass from* BARBARA): Let me get you some ginger ale.

BARBARA *(Pulling away):* But I'd rather have wine.

ERIC *(Firmly):* No, you wouldn't.

MILO (*Moving in front of* ERIC): Yes, she would. (*Handing glass of wine to* MURIEL)

MURIEL: Your brother's gone to a lot of trouble, Eric.

MILO *(Casually):* All in a night's work. (MURIEL *takes a sip. Others watch intently.*)

ERIC: How is it?

MURIEL *(Taking another sip):* Interesting. Where did you get it from?

MILO *(Pleasantly):* Where or whom?

MURIEL *(Puzzled):* I beg your pardon?

ERIC: He means it was a present.

MILO: You might say that. (BARBARA *sips, makes face.*)

MURIEL: How nice. *(Takes another sip)* This is interesting, isn't it, Barbara?

BARBARA *(Awkwardly):* I'm . . . really not much of a wine drinker, Milo.

ERIC *(Snatching her glass away):* Great! I'll get you a ginger ale. *(Exits left)*

BARBARA (*To* MILO): Eric didn't tell me he has a younger brother.

MILO *(Setting bottle down):* He doesn't. I'm older.

MURIEL *(Surprised):* Granted, you're quite mature. But you can't be older.

MILO: Of course I can. You'd be surprised how old I am.

MURIEL: Let me guess. Twenty-four?

MILO *(Laughing):* You're off by a hundred.

MURIEL *(Laughing nervously):* Seriously.

MILO: I *was* serious. *(Shrugs)* At least I think it's a hundred. I stopped counting a few years ago.

MURIEL *(Laughing):* Didn't we all?

BARBARA: What do you do?

MILO: About what?

BARBARA: About work.

MILO: I hang around the house a lot.

BARBARA *(Concerned):* You're unemployed?

MURIEL *(Taking* MILO's *arm):* She's not always this direct, Milo. She just wants to know she's marrying into a good family. Good bloodlines, and all.

ERIC (*Re-entering with glass of ginger ale for* BARBARA): What's going on?

BARBARA *(Casually):* They're just talking about bloodlines.

ERIC *(In a panic):* Oh, no! *(Rushes over to* MILO *and takes his arm)* I hate to break this up, Milo, but I know how you hate to be late.

MILO: For what?

ERIC: Didn't you tell me you had to be somewhere?

MILO: Not until sunrise.

ERIC: Well, this way you can get an early start. *(Pushing him upstage)*

MURIEL *(Upset):* You're not leaving us so soon, are you, Milo?

MILO *(Returning):* Oh, no—not if you insist.

ERIC *(Between clenched teeth):* Milo!

MURIEL: I was hoping I'd get a tour of the house.

MILO *(Extending his arm):* Allow me to escort you. (MURIEL *giggles and takes his arm.*) We'll start with the cellar.

ERIC: Why don't you start with the attic?

MILO: I was going to show her the pool table.

ERIC: The view's better from the attic.

MILO: Muriel, have you ever seen real bats in a belfry? We have some. *(As they exit)* Come on!

BARBARA (*Crossing to* ERIC): Eric, what's wrong with you?

ERIC: Nothing.

BARBARA: You're being terrible to your brother. He's obviously only trying to make a good impression.

ERIC: But your mother—

BARBARA: She's crazy about him. Granted, he's kind of strange—

ERIC: That's putting it mildly.

BARBARA: Is there something you're not telling me?

ERIC: I think you'd better sit down. *(She crosses to chair and sits.)*

BARBARA: Well?

ERIC: It's about Milo.

BARBARA: What about him?

ERIC *(Awkwardly):* I don't know how you're going to feel about this, Barbara, but . . . *(Sighs)* He's going to be living here with us after we're married.

BARBARA: Because he's unemployed?

ERIC: What makes you say that?

BARBARA: He said he just hangs around.

ERIC: What he *meant* was that—(BARBARA *is listening intently.* ERIC *tries another tack.)* Did you know he wants to come to the wedding? (MILO *re-enters upstage, out of breath.* BARBARA *and* ERIC *don't notice him;* MILO *eavesdrops on the conversation.)*

BARBARA: I was expecting that he would. Isn't it some kind of tradition to have your brother as your best man?

ERIC: He wants the wedding at night.

BARBARA: An evening wedding's fine with me.

ERIC *(Looking at her):* Midnight.

BARBARA *(Puzzled):* Midnight?

ERIC: I knew you'd hate it.

BARBARA: I don't *hate* it. It's just sort of an unusual time to get married, isn't it?

ERIC: Milo can't come to the wedding unless it's at midnight.

BARBARA *(Rising and crossing to put her arms around* ERIC): Well, if it's that important to you, Eric, it's fine with me.

ERIC: Is it? (MILO *is pleased with the news.*)

BARBARA: I love you. *(Shrugs)* Besides, we'll beat all the traffic on the way to the lake. (ERIC *is still downcast.*) Is that what was bothering you?

ERIC *(Breaking away from her):* You're going to have to find out sooner or later.

BARBARA: Find out what?

ERIC: About the wine . . . and the flowers . . . and about Milo.

BARBARA *(Disturbed):* What about them?

ERIC *(Sighing deeply):* Barbara, my ancestors left Bavaria to get *away* from something.

BARBARA: Like taxes?

ERIC: Like—a curse. *(Pause)* Every other generation gets it.

BARBARA: A curse?

ERIC: The only problem is, it followed them here.

BARBARA: The curse?

ERIC: Yes.

BARBARA: Eric, are you saying that Milo has it?

ERIC *(Relieved):* Yes.

BARBARA: Well, what kind of curse is it?

ERIC: The curse, Barbara, is—

MILO *(Stepping forward):* The Curse of the Bard. *(Taking* BARBARA's *hand)* Forgive the ramblings of an embarrassed heir. It pains Eric to speak of it.

BARBARA: Will someone please tell me what's going on here?

ERIC: Milo—

MILO (*To* ERIC): She has to know the truth, straight from the lips of a man who has lived his life in shadow and deception. *(Holds hand up in warning)* You must swear never to reveal what I am about to tell you.

ERIC *(Sullenly):* Who'd believe her if she did?

BARBARA *(Interested):* What is it, Milo?

MILO *(With pride):* You see before you . . . *(Dramatically)* an actor! (ERIC *does a double-take.*)

BARBARA *(Impressed):* An actor?

MILO: Sh-h-h! No one must know.

BARBARA (*To* ERIC): Is that what you were trying to tell me? (ERIC *shrugs and laughs nervously.*)

MILO *(Pacing):* I have been cursed from birth to tread upon the stage, to smell the greasepaint . . . to revel in the roar of a crowd . . . to suffer the slings and arrows of outrageous fortune. . . .

BARBARA: How come you don't have the curse too, Eric?

ERIC: No talent, I guess.

BARBARA *(Puzzled):* Then, Milo, do you mean you're the black sheep of the family?

MILO: Yes. And for that reason, no one must ever be told how I spend my days.

BARBARA: So *that's* why you want an evening wedding—because you have daytime rehearsals!

MILO: That's it exactly! (ERIC *sighs with relief.*)

BARBARA *(Excitedly):* Maybe we could come and see you perform some time.

MILO *(With a smile):* Or perhaps I could bring my

friends home . . . if Eric has no objections.

ERIC *(Forced to comply):* Any time you'd like.

BARBARA *(Looking around):* By the way, where's Mother?

MILO: Taking herself on the tour. *(Waving his hand)* Perhaps you'd like to join her.

BARBARA: Good idea. She'll probably get lost. *(Kisses* ERIC) Call me when dinner's ready. *(Starts to exit)* Oh—what were you going to tell me about the wine and flowers?

ERIC: Uh—*(Shrugs)* I forget. (BARBARA *exits.* ERIC *addresses* MILO.) An *actor?*

MILO: She believed it, didn't she? *(Pause)* She's really a very nice girl.

ERIC *(After a moment):* Do you think we should tell her the rest?

MILO: No—I think you should quit while you're ahead. *(Starting to exit)* Let me know how dinner turns out.

ERIC: You're not staying?

MILO *(Shuddering):* I can't run the risk of sitting next to Barbara's mother.

ERIC *(Suddenly curious):* Hey, what happened? Weren't you showing her the house?

MILO: I was . . . until she told me about her volunteer work at the church.

ERIC: I see. I know it's not one of your best subjects.

MILO: And do you know what she wears around her neck and almost *showed* me?

ERIC *(Stifling a laugh):* I hope you were polite.

MILO (*Shrugging*): When you've seen one, you've seen 'em all. (*Turns to exit*)

ERIC (*Awkwardly*): I—uh—really appreciate what you did tonight . . . Dad. You know, we live in different worlds, but you're still my father, and I'm grateful for your help tonight.

MILO (*Without turning around*): Don't mention it, son.

ERIC: There is one thing I'm wondering about, though. . . . If the curse is on every other generation, and Barbara and I have children . . . (MILO *turns around to reveal vampire fangs.*) Oh, never mind. (*Waves*) Goodnight, Dad—and thanks. (MILO *waves goodbye. Curtain*)

THE END

PRODUCTION NOTES

SHADOW OF DRACULA

Characters: 2 male; 2 female.

Playing Time: 30 minutes.

Costumes: Milo wears black vest and slacks, white shirt, red bow tie, floor length black cape. Eric, slacks, long-sleeved shirt, tie. Barbara and Muriel, dressy evening attire.

Properties: Wine glasses, flowers, tomato juice in opaque wine bottle.

Setting: Gothic mansion. Fireplace is up right. Table with wine glasses is downstage right. Two chairs are downstage left. Skull is on mantel.

The Curse of Cassandra

Characters

WAYNE NESBITT
PETRA NIKALOVIAS

TIME: *Present; a summer evening.*

SETTING: *Wayne's apartment. Couch, center, has in front of it a coffee table with box of crackers and large ashtray on it. Small table, with phone, directory, and envelope on it, and a few chairs complete the furnishings.*

AT RISE: WAYNE *hastily enters, buttoning shirt cuffs, and crosses to phone. He dials anxiously.*

WAYNE *(Quickly; into phone):* Hello, Mrs. Stillwell. . . . *(Frowns)* This is Wayne. . . . Wayne Nesbitt . . . *(Nodding slowly)* That's right—your daughter's boyfriend. . . . I know. . . . Someone's parked right behind my car, and I can't get out until I find the manager! . . . *(Insisting)* I would take a cab, but they're all on strike. . . . Just go ahead with dinner. . . . Could I talk to Nancy for a second? . . . Thanks. . . . Hello, Nancy? . . . I'm running a little late. . . . *(Irritably)* I know your first pot roast is a big occasion, but I can't get my car out. . . . *(Doorbell rings.)* There's the door— can you hold on a minute? . . . *(Frowns)* Oh, Mrs. Stillwell. . . . *(Looks anxiously at front door)* I didn't say anything to upset her! . . . . Of course I love her. . . . *(Doorbell rings again; hastily)* Mrs. Stillwell, there's someone at the door—probably my manager. Let me just say goodbye to Nancy. . . . Nancy? I'll call you back, O.K.? *(Doorbell rings three times in rapid succession; he holds hand over mouthpiece and yells.)* Come on in—it's open! *(Into phone)* Nancy, I have to go. (PETRA *enters cautiously;* WAYNE *doesn't notice her at first; into phone)* My apartment manager— who else? *(Turns and sees* PETRA; *he stammers hastily into phone)* Nancy, I'll see you soon, O.K.? Bye! (*Hangs up and stares at* PETRA)

PETRA *(Smiling):* Hi! *(Noticing* WAYNE's *quizzical look)* You were expecting me, weren't you?

WAYNE *(Nodding uncertainly):* I think so. *(Suspiciously)* Who are you?

PETRA *(Somewhat miffed):* You mean they didn't tell you my name?

WAYNE *(Awkwardly):* They said they were sending someone—they just didn't say it was you.

PETRA *(Extending her hand):* Well, I'm Petra

Nikalovias. *(Shakes his hand)* It's hard to pronounce, so that's probably why they wanted me to introduce myself. And you must be Wayne.

WAYNE: That's right.

PETRA *(Admiring the apartment):* Nice place you have.

WAYNE: Thanks.

PETRA: So, where are we going?

WAYNE *(Puzzled):* I thought we'd start with the garage, since that's where the car is.

PETRA *(Laughing):* I mean after that, where are we going?

WAYNE *(Uncertainly):* Going for what?

PETRA: For our first date!

WAYNE *(Scratching his head):* Uh—I think you have the wrong address.

PETRA: I don't think so. *(Rummages quickly in purse and withdraws slip of paper; reading from slip)* This is 2643 Jennings Drive, #4B, isn't it?

WAYNE *(Nodding):* Yes.

PETRA: And it's June 14th?

WAYNE: Right.

PETRA: Eight o'clock?

WAYNE *(Looking at watch):* Yes—eight o'clock on the nose. (PETRA *thrusts note back into her purse.*)

PETRA *(Satisfied):* Then there's no mistake. You're Wayne Carlisle, and we have a date!

WAYNE *(Quickly):* Stop right there! You see, I'm not Wayne Carlisle. I'm Wayne Nesbitt.

PETRA: Then who's Wayne Carlisle?

WAYNE *(Shrugging):* I have no idea.

PETRA: But you're in his apartment. *(Suspiciously)* Are you sure he's not your roommate or something?

WAYNE: No. I've been here for three years. If someone else were living here, I think I would have noticed by now.

PETRA: How strange. *(Pauses)* Are you sure you weren't expecting me? I mean, you said yourself you were expecting someone, right?

WAYNE: Yes, my apartment manager was supposed to send someone over.

PETRA: I was sent here by Compu-Date, Inc.

WAYNE: Never heard of them.

PETRA: It's a computer dating service where you *(Accusingly)*—alias Wayne Carlisle—filled out an application and questionnaire for the best date of your life.

WAYNE *(Folding his arms):* The plot thickens.

PETRA *(Continuing):* Yesterday afternoon at 4:27 your computer application card and mine came out of the same slot.

WAYNE: And what does that mean?

PETRA: It means that I'm the girl you've been waiting for!

WAYNE: You are?

PETRA: If you weren't looking for someone like me, why did you fill out the questionnaire?

WAYNE: But I've never filled out an application for a date.

PETRA: Can you prove it? *(Pauses)* Because if you

can't, I'm going to demand a refund! (WAYNE *crosses to table, left, picks up envelope, removes card and hands it to her.)*

WAYNE: This should explain everything.

PETRA *(Reading):* "The Gordon Stillwells of Rockingham Place cordially invite you to the occasion of their daughter Nancy's first culinary endeavor." *(Looks up)* Culinary endeavor?

WAYNE: Nancy's my girlfriend. She's fixing a pot roast.

PETRA: So? *(Reading)* "The 14th of June at 8 p.m." *(Looks up)* Hm-m-m. I see.

WAYNE: It's already after eight, and . . .

PETRA *(Looking at her watch):* And you're going to be late.

WAYNE *(Escorting her to door):* And so, Miss Whoever-You-Are, much as I've enjoyed this, you'll have to go.

PETRA *(With a dramatic sigh):* What a shame. *(Leaning limply in doorway)* I was really looking forward to dinner. I'm starved.

WAYNE *(Shrugging):* What can I say?

PETRA: Well, you could say, "May I offer you something to eat?"

WAYNE: And what if I don't?

PETRA: Then it's entirely likely that I will faint in your doorway, which you may find rather difficult to explain to your neighbors.

WAYNE: Oh. *(Pauses thoughtfully as* PETRA *steps into room again and closes door behind her)* O.K.

What would you like to eat?

PETRA: What do you have?

WAYNE *(Scratching his head):* Well . . . *(Looks around, sees box of crackers, and picks them up)* Crackers?

PETRA: You certainly lead a Spartan life!

WAYNE: Well . . . *(Looks around for a bowl; empties crackers into ashtray)* I eat out a lot. *(Crosses to pick up another chair and moves it to table)*

PETRA *(Taking cracker and nibbling on it):* That can get expensive. You must have a good job. *(Curiously)* What exactly do you do, anyway?

WAYNE *(Shrugging):* Oh, it's not important.

PETRA *(Sitting):* I'll tell you what I do if you tell me what you do.

WAYNE: I don't remember asking you.

PETRA: I'll tell you anyway. *(Pleased)* I tell fortunes.

WAYNE: For a living?

PETRA: No, for fun. For a living, I'm a clerk typist. Now it's your turn.

WAYNE *(Uneasily):* I'm . . . a writer.

PETRA *(Surprised):* Really? I've never met a writer before! *(Pauses)* Have I read anything you've written?

WAYNE: I don't know. What have you read?

PETRA *(Thinking): Gone With the Wind* . . . *Dr. Zhivago* . . . *Jaws.* . . .

WAYNE: Sorry. I didn't write any of those.

PETRA: What have you written?

WAYNE *(Awkwardly):* Have you ever heard of the Bronze Tiger or the Fern Garden?

PETRA: No. Are those the names of your books?

WAYNE: Not exactly. *(Pauses)* They're the names of restaurants.

PETRA *(Puzzled):* You write about restaurants?

WAYNE *(Explaining): For* restaurants.

PETRA: I don't understand.

WAYNE: I write menus.

PETRA *(Laughing):* You're kidding! *(Takes another cracker)* Seriously, what do you do?

WAYNE: I really do write menus. My descriptions make the dishes sound inviting.

PETRA: You mean the succulent sauces and crunchy salads and irresistible soup de jour—that's all yours?

WAYNE *(Defensively):* Everyone has to start somewhere.

PETRA: How long have you been doing this?

WAYNE: Oh . . . a couple of years. It may all change after Saturday, though.

PETRA: What happens Saturday? Are they making one of your specialties into a movie?

WAYNE *(Annoyed):* I hope you realize that it would never have worked out between the two of us, Petula.

PETRA *(Wryly):* Especially since you can't even remember my name. It's Petra.

WAYNE *(Shrugging):* Sorry. Anyway, to answer your question, I'm sort of considering proposing to Nancy Stillwell on Saturday.

PETRA *(Puzzled):* Why does that name sound familiar?

WAYNE *(Pointing to the invitation):* Dinner, remember?

PETRA: Ah, yes—the culinary endeavor. So she's won you over with pot roast, and you're going to propose.

WAYNE: Well, I'm not sure. *(Pauses)* I mean, I'm not even sure if her father likes me yet, and her mother keeps forgetting my name.

PETRA: Isn't it more important that Nancy like you? Do you like her? Why are you worried about her father?

WAYNE: You see, he owns the Bronze Tiger and the Fern Garden.

PETRA: Ah! Now I see.

WAYNE *(Rising and pacing):* Well, if I stop seeing Nancy I could lose my job. *(Shrugs)* Nancy thought it would be nice if I went to work for her father. I might even get a promotion—that would mean I could quit writing menus.

PETRA: If you ask me, marriage is a pretty big step if all you're after is full-time employment.

WAYNE *(Defensively):* Don't get me wrong. Nancy's a nice girl, and we're going to have a good life together. *(Earnestly)* I do love her—I think.

PETRA: Are you trying to convince me or yourself?

WAYNE *(Scratching his head):* Why would I do that? I don't even know you.

PETRA: If you have a problem, maybe I can help you out.

WAYNE: Thanks, but I don't have any problems.

PETRA *(Wistfully):* You're lucky. *(Sighing)* I wish I could say the same.

WAYNE *(Curiously):* Why? What's wrong in your life?

PETRA *(Picking up her purse and rising):* Oh, it's nothing really. *(Heading for door)* I've taken enough of your time as it is.

WAYNE: Look, I can't go anywhere till someone gets my car. Can you at least give me a hint about what's bothering you?

PETRA *(Shaking her head):* It's a long story.

WAYNE *(Checking his watch):* Well, can you put it in 25 words or less?

PETRA *(Shrugging):* I could put it in four, but you'd only laugh.

WAYNE: I promise not to laugh.

PETRA *(Taking a deep breath):* I'm . . . under a curse.

WAYNE *(Confused):* A what?

PETRA: A curse.

WAYNE *(Nodding uncertainly):* That's what I thought you said.

PETRA *(Walking toward him):* You don't believe me, do you?

WAYNE *(Stepping back):* Of course I do! *(Laughs nervously; tries to regain his composure)* How long has this curse been going on?

PETRA *(Sighing):* All my life. It's the Curse of Cassandra. *(Pauses)* Do you know who Cassandra was?

WAYNE: No, but I'm sure you'll tell me.

PETRA: Well, Cassandra was a Trojan princess who learned from Apollo how to predict the future. *(Pauses)* There was a catch, though.

WAYNE: What? That she was always wrong?

PETRA: No . . . she was always *right*!

WAYNE: Then what was the problem?

PETRA: The curse was that no one would ever believe her.

WAYNE: What does this have to do with you?

PETRA: I have the same gift she had. The curse of prophecy.

WAYNE: Is it contagious?

PETRA *(Impatiently):* Of course not, but I'm doomed to have it the rest of my life unless the right person comes along.

WAYNE *(To himself):* Why am I intrigued by this?

PETRA: That's why I was looking forward to this date. I asked to meet someone who believed in astrology.

WAYNE: How could that help?

PETRA *(Shrugging):* My plan was to tell his fortune. If he believed in my prediction and followed my advice, the curse on me would be broken.

WAYNE *(With sudden resolution):* Why don't you tell my fortune? Not that I'd take it seriously or anything—it would just be to help you out.

PETRA: Why would I want to do that? You've as much as told me that your future is already taken care of.

WAYNE (*Struggling*): Whatever you have to add should only confirm what I already know, right? (*Pauses*) I'll tell you I believe you, and we can go our separate ways. End of curse.

PETRA: It wouldn't work unless you took me seriously.

WAYNE: Try me—you have nothing to lose.

PETRA (*Sighing*): Well, if you insist. (*Takes deck of cards from purse, shuffles them, and holds them out to* WAYNE) Pick three cards. (*With great forethought, he selects three cards and hands them to her. She puts rest of deck down and studies the three carefully.*) Hm-m-m.

WAYNE (*Impatiently*): Well?

PETRA (*Nodding*): I can see you're very much in love with her (*Looking at him*)—the girl you're going to marry is quite attractive.

WAYNE: You're right so far.

PETRA: But you have to be careful—redheads can be temperamental.

WAYNE (*Surprised*): Redhead? No, that's not right. Nancy's blonde.

PETRA: I'm only reading what's in the cards. The girl you're going to marry is a redhead.

WAYNE: But that's ridiculous! I don't even know a redhead. . . . (*Stops and reflects a moment*)

PETRA: Something wrong?

WAYNE *(Casually):* I was just going to say I *used* to know a redhead . . . *(Nervously)* a long time ago. Before I ever met Nancy.

PETRA *(Studying cards):* Did her name start with a "J"?

WAYNE *(Nodding; startled):* Yes, as a matter of fact—"J" for Jamie. *(Pointing to cards)* Is that in there?

PETRA *(Continuing):* You were going to get married . . . but it didn't work out.

WAYNE *(Musing):* Funny, I haven't thought about that for years.

PETRA *(Looking up):* You'd better start thinking about it now.

WAYNE *(Puzzled):* Why should I? It's been over for ages.

PETRA: She's coming back into your life—tonight.

WAYNE *(Upset):* But that's impossible.

PETRA *(Sighing):* The cards never lie. *(Scowling as she looks at cards)* You'll meet at a restaurant. Italian, I think. *(Looks up)* The name is "Mario's Gondola." Ever hear of it?

WAYNE *(Amazed):* Why, that was Jamie's favorite place! Oh, this is really ridiculous! *(Pauses)* Besides, she's probably married, has three kids and lives in Ashtabula, right?

PETRA *(Shaking her head):* She's never married.

WAYNE *(Incredulously):* She hasn't?

PETRA: She's always been in love with you. She'll never change.

WAYNE *(Sadly):* Well, I've always been in love with her, too, but I had to be practical.

PETRA: Practical?

WAYNE *(Shrugging):* What kind of life could I give her as a menu writer? I may be 109 before I write my first best-selling novel!

PETRA: And how long would it take you to write your best seller if you married Nancy Stillwell?

WAYNE *(Shaking his head):* I guess I probably never would. Nancy thinks writing is sort of silly. She doesn't believe I could ever get a novel published. That's why she wants me to work for her father.

PETRA: And what did Jamie think?

WAYNE *(Smiling):* Jamie said I wrote some of the best menus in town. She used to tell all her friends to go to the restaurants whenever they added a new specialty to the menu. Not because the cooking was that good, but because the description of it was worth a standing ovation. *(Dreamily)* She always believed in me. . . .

PETRA *(Picking up her things):* Well, you asked for a glimpse of the future. *(Hands him cards)* What more can I say?

WAYNE *(Musing):* It would be nice seeing Jamie again, but . . . how do I know it would work out?

PETRA: You don't—no more than you know it would work out with Nancy. *(Points to cards again)* At least with Jamie you'd know that fate was on your side.

WAYNE *(Sighing):* I don't even know why I'm thinking about it—it's too ridiculous ever to come true.

PETRA: Why?

WAYNE: How could Jamie possibly come back into
my life tonight? The last I heard she moved to
Cleveland. What would she be doing here? And
what chance is there that I'd run into her again?
And what about Nancy and her pot roast?

PETRA *(Wryly):* You're certainly agonizing a lot
over something you don't believe in.

WAYNE: What if—strictly to satisfy my curiosity, of
course—I called the restaurant?

PETRA: What for?

WAYNE: To prove to you—and to myself—that she's
not there. I'm afraid it wouldn't help fix your
curse of Cassandra, but I'd like to make sure
Jamie isn't at the restaurant.

PETRA *(Shrugging):* You could try, I suppose.

WAYNE *(Crossing to phone):* I'll call the restaurant
and ask if she's there. *(Picks up directory, looks
up number)* And then they'll say she's not, and I
can forget this whole business—Cassandra and
you and Jamie—once and for all. *(Dials; into
phone)* Hello. Is this Mario's Gondola? . . . Mario
himself? . . . Well, how are you, Mario? This is
Wayne Nesbitt. You probably don't remember
me, but . . . *(Pleased)* Yes, that's right—the vel-
vety marinara and parmesan of Olympus. Yes, it
has been a long time. . . . Uh-huh. Listen, Mario,
do you remember the girl I used to date—really

pretty, long red hair, and—*(Mouth drops open in amazement)* What do you mean, "Do I want to talk to her?" You mean she's there? *(To* PETRA*)* She's there! *(Into phone)* No, that's O.K. Thanks, Mario. *(Hangs up)*

PETRA: So she's there, huh?

WAYNE *(With a casual shrug):* It's probably just a coincidence. Mario probably made a mistake.

PETRA: So much for my dinner. *(Heads for exit)*

WAYNE: Where are you going?

PETRA: Home.

WAYNE *(Awkwardly):* You're not . . . going by Mario's Gondola on 43rd, are you?

PETRA *(Slyly):* Why?

WAYNE: I just thought that—if you were—I could ride along with you.

PETRA: But you just said that Mario could have made a mistake.

WAYNE: There is a remote possibility that my favorite person in the whole world could be sitting at a table in what was our favorite restaurant.

PETRA: And if she's not there?

WAYNE: Then I'll walk over to Nancy's. *(Looks at watch)* If I hurry, I can still make dessert. *(Shakes head)* Why am I doing this? It's almost as if I want her to be there.

PETRA *(Smiling):* Shall we go? *(Takes keys out of purse)*

WAYNE *(Shrugging):* Sure. *(They start to exit; suddenly she stops)*

PETRA: Hey—I just remembered something. Mind if I use your phone a second?

WAYNE: Go ahead.

PETRA *(Crossing to phone):* I promised my mother I'd pick up some groceries on the way home. This'll only take a second. *(Tosses him the keys)* Why don't you get the car started? I'll be right down. *(Dials)*

WAYNE: Where are you parked?

PETRA *(Dialing):* Downstairs, in the garage. I know it's for tenants of the building, but I didn't think they'd mind. It's a yellow Datsun.

WAYNE: So that's your car!

PETRA *(Enthusiastically; into phone):* Hi, Mama! Did you have a good day? *(With a shrug,* WAYNE *exits.)* I'm on my way home—is there something special you'd like at the store? *(When* WAYNE *is gone, she hangs up quickly, checks the directory and re-dials. Into phone)* Hello, Mario's? . . . I wonder if you could call someone to the phone for me. It's the Reynolds reservation—party of one. . . . Thank you. *(Pauses, then starts grinning)* Hi, Jamie. It's all taken care of. We'll be there in about ten minutes. . . . Uh-huh. . . . *(Smiles)* Hey, what are best friends for? . . . You'll never believe the story I had to tell him! *(Laughs)* All I did was give fate a little helping hand. *(Quick curtain)*

THE END

PRODUCTION NOTES

THE CURSE OF CASSANDRA

Characters: 1 female; 1 male.

Playing Time: 25 minutes.

Costumes: Wayne and Petra wear dressy clothes. Wayne wears watch; Petra carries purse containing slip of paper, deck of cards and keys.

Properties: Paper; cards; keys.

Setting: Wayne's apartment. Couch is center; in front of it stands coffee table with box of crackers and large ashtray. A few chairs and a small table, with telephone, directory, and envelope on it, complete the furnishings. Right wall has working door.

Lighting: No special effects.

Sound: Doorbell.

Dateline: Romance

Characters

ERIK BOWMAN
HILARY BRANDT
WAITER

TIME: *An evening in the present.*

SETTING: *Quiet French restaurant. Table, vase with rose in it, and two chairs are center. Table is set with dinner plates and silverware.*

AT RISE: ERIK *and* HILARY, *seated at table, have just finished eating dinner.* WAITER *enters and approaches table.*

WAITER *(With French accent):* The meal—was it satisfactory?

ERIK: Great!

HILARY: Yes, it was excellent. Although the portions did seem a little smaller than the last time I was here.

WAITER *(With short laugh):* Merely, mademoiselle, an optical illusion.

HILARY: Oh? How is that?

WAITER *(Indicating the room):* The restaurant has been enlarged, so the portions *seem* smaller.

HILARY *(Dubiously):* That's an interesting explanation.

WAITER *(Handing* ERIK *a small menu):* The dessert list, monsieur?

ERIK: Would you like dessert, Hilary?

HILARY: Whatever you're having will be fine.

ERIK *(Handing it back to* WAITER): Two "Jacques Bonapartes" and coffee.

WAITER *(Patiently):* Jacques Bonaparte, monsieur, is the owner of the restaurant. *(Pointing to menu)* The desserts are on this side. (ERIK *looks perplexed as he tries to read them, then shakes his head, hands menu back.)*

ERIK: What do you recommend?

WAITER: The specials are magnifique, monsieur. *(Describing them with gusto)* Chocolat pièce de résistance, Creme de la Antoinette—

HILARY: How about something simple—like vanilla ice cream?

WAITER *(With exaggerated dignity):* Surely mademoiselle is joking.

ERIK *(Dismissing him with a gesture):* We'll just have coffee. Thank you. (WAITER *nods and exits.)*

HILARY *(Laughing):* Jacques Bonaparte?

ERIK *(With a laugh):* It takes a lot of nerve to admit

that the only word you recognize on the menu is "menu."

HILARY: Serves you right for flunking French.

ERIK: I'll do better next time. You'll see.

HILARY: Next time?

ERIK: Yes. *(Imitating* WAITER*)* You could try the snails nested on a bed of watercress with dressing. . . .

HILARY: There is no "next time" on my calendar. We have nothing in common.

ERIK: With snails or with each other?

HILARY *(Smiling):* You really are impossible.

ERIK *(Lightly):* But not without charm, right? *(Pauses)* Aren't you having any fun with me?

HILARY *(Sighing):* Let's just say this wasn't exactly what I expected.

ERIK: Hmm . . . are you sure it wasn't just the perch crêpes in orange sauce?

HILARY *(Slowly, smiling):* The waiter *did* say it was an excellent choice.

ERIK *(Laughing):* I'm sure he says that about everything. *(Pretending to order)* I think I'll have the breadsticks sauteed in spiced yogurt, with a sprig of fresh parsley. *(Imitating* WAITER*)* An excellent choice, monsieur. They go to foreign waiters' school to get their accents, you know. They're really all ᶠrom Ohio.

HILARY: Really? Well, at least the service was good.

ERIK *(Airily):* Ah—modern technology, microwave ovens. *(Sighs)* Where will it all end?

HILARY *(Abruptly):* Enough of that, now. And besides, I'm growing more curious—and impatient—by the minute.

ERIK: About what?

HILARY *(Reminding him):* You said you'd give me the answer to my question after dinner, and it's after dinner.

ERIK: So is 1997. So is 2049. Besides, it's not officially "after dinner" until the coffee arrives. *(WAITER enters with tray on which there are two cups of coffee.)*

WAITER: Coffee, monsieur. *(Puts cups on table)* Will there be anything else?

ERIK: Just the check, please.

WAITER *(Taking check from pocket):* As you wish, monsieur. *(Puts it on table)* I'll take it when you're ready. *(Exits)*

ERIK *(Looking at check; aghast):* Do you think he'd mind coming back in about thirty years?

HILARY: Well, Erik, now that it's officially after dinner, you can answer my question.

ERIK: What was it again?

HILARY: For someone who seems to distrust computers, why would you let one pick a date for you? All I want is a simple answer.

ERIK *(Thinking a moment, then responding):* Because . . .

HILARY: Because why?

ERIK: You got your simple answer. A complex answer will cost you another dinner.

HILARY: Erik, are you hiding something?

ERIK: Me? *(With a nervous laugh)* Of course not! It's just that it's a secret that I wouldn't share with just anyone. If you were to whisper a word to anyone—

HILARY: My lips are sealed.

ERIK: Not officially, they're not. *(Lightly)* Rule Number Three of the official handbook of lip-sealing requires that be done with a kiss.

HILARY *(Wryly):* Is that a fact?

ERIK *(With mock seriousness):* Definitely. Regulation 641379, Article 27, Paragraph 4, Line 13. Oldest rule in the book.

HILARY: Then why isn't it Number One?

ERIK *(Leaning over to kiss her):* Are you absolutely sure you want to know?

HILARY: Oh, Erik! I wish you'd stop being so evasive!

ERIK: All right, I'll tell you. I guess I should have from the very beginning.

HILARY: What's the big deal about telling me why you let a computer find you a date?

ERIK *(Shrugging):* Nothing, I suppose. *(Pauses)* The truth is, Hilary, that I did it for the same reason that you did. *(Pauses)* Why did *you* do it?

HILARY: Curiosity.

ERIK: Ah—but curiosity killed many a romance.

HILARY: I thought it killed only cats.

ERIK: Yes, but cats have nine lives.

HILARY: And romance?

ERIK: It depends on whether you believe in reincarnation.

HILARY: Do you?

ERIK *(Nodding):* Absolutely. In my last life, I was a Brontosaurus.

HILARY: What took you so long to come back?

ERIK: I knew that this was the year I'd meet you. *(She smiles.)*

HILARY: Come on, now, Erik. . . .

ERIK: Well, I guess the best place to start is to tell you I'm a writer.

HILARY *(Sarcastically):* Of what—dime novels?

ERIK: When I sell ten, I'll have a dollar.

HILARY: Don't spend it all in one place. *(Looks at her watch)* Hey, I have to be going pretty soon, Erik. I've got a big day tomorrow.

ERIK: The busses have stopped running.

HILARY: I'll call a cab.

ERIK: Why call a cab when I have a waiting chariot?

HILARY *(Rising):* Thanks anyway. *(Puts out hand)* I've enjoyed our dinner.

ERIK: Gosh, I guess I can't stall any longer. Hilary, there's something I have to tell you before you go. *(Hesitates)* Only . . .

HILARY: Only what? *(Sits)*

ERIK: I'm not sure how you're going to take this, but I'm . . . well, I'm not exactly what I seem.

HILARY: Oh?

ERIK: Well, Hilary, I've been . . . *(Abruptly)* What was that?

HILARY *(Nervously):* What was what?

ERIK: That clicking sound.

HILARY *(Blandly):* I didn't hear a thing.

ERIK: I'm sure it came from your purse.

HILARY *(Laughing nervously):* My purse? Don't be silly! (ERIK *reaches into her handbag and withdraws a small tape recorder.*)

ERIK: Do you always carry a tape recorder in your purse?

HILARY *(In mock surprise):* Now, how did that get in there? (ERIK *hits "play" button and the last part of their conversation plays back.*)

ERIK *(Angrily):* I know I'm a sparkling conversationalist, but no one's ever thought I was worth recording.

HILARY *(Sheepishly):* I guess you'd like an explanation, huh?

ERIK: In twenty-five words or less.

HILARY *(Sighing):* If only it were that simple. You see, Erik . . . I'm not what you think I am. I only filled in "secretary" as my occupation on the computer date card, but . . .

ERIK *(Upset; interrupting):* But what are you then?

HILARY: I hope you don't hate me, Erik, but I'm a reporter.

ERIK *(Coolly):* Why should I hate you because you're a reporter?

HILARY: Because you're sort of an assignment for me.

ERIK: An assignment?

HILARY *(Shrugging):* I thought it would be kind of a lark to write about people who go to computer dating services, and I wanted to hear it first hand.

ERIK *(Coolly):* So . . . you weren't serious about anything you've said.

HILARY *(Embarrassed):* Actually, it all turned out differently from what I planned. I mean I imagined it would just be another story but we've had such a good time that—

ERIK: That what?

HILARY: That I realized I couldn't write the story, and *(Sadly)* I can't see you again, either. *(Sighs, as* ERIK *doesn't respond)* How was I to know that I'd end up liking the person the computer matched me with?

ERIK: Shouldn't that tell you something?

HILARY *(Unhappily):* What? I made up my whole biography!

ERIK *(Handing her the recorder):* It wouldn't have made any difference, Hilary. We would have met anyway.

HILARY *(Puzzled):* I don't understand.

ERIK *(A bit sheepishly):* Let me fill in a few blanks of my own. To begin with, there's my occupation.

HILARY: You mean you're not really a writer?

ERIK: Oh, I'm a writer, all right. But I don't write novels. I write restaurant critiques for a newspaper you may have heard of. *The Tribune.*

HILARY *(Astounded): The Tribune*? But I work for *The Tribune*!

ERIK: Exactly. You're on the second floor and I'm on the fourth.

HILARY *(Suspiciously):* Wait a minute. That can't be right. I happen to know for a fact that *The Tribune* has had the same food editor for three years—a woman named Sonia Something-or-Other.

ERIK: Applebaum.

HILARY: Yes, that's it!

ERIK *(Shaking her hand):* Pleased to meet you.

HILARY *(Puzzled):* I don't get it.

ERIK: I'm the best-kept secret at *The Tribune*, Hilary. And, besides, the best-kept secret from the restaurants I review. I owe my readers an impartial opinion, so I masquerade as an ordinary customer. . . .

HILARY: Who can't pronounce entrees on the menu, hm-m-m? But the computer dating service, our getting together—

ERIK: All the ingredients of a delicious mystery, Hilary. To tell you the truth, I asked the kid who brings you your jelly doughnuts in the morning, to leave the classified ad idea on your desk in the hope that you'd pursue it.

HILARY: But how did you know I wouldn't be matched with someone else?

ERIK *(Embarrassed):* I have to confess. My best friend runs the service. He knew how much I wanted to meet you, so he made sure our cards came out the same slot. (HILARY *stands.*)

HILARY (*Sarcastically*): So what's next on the agenda, Sonia?

ERIK: Would you care to join me in a dish of ice cream? (*He stands and takes her hand.*) I know a great ice cream parlor that serves things I can pronounce. (*They laugh and exit togther, hand in hand. Curtain*)

THE END

PRODUCTION NOTES

DATELINE: ROMANCE

Characters: 2 male; 1 female.

Playing Time: 10 minutes.

Costume: Modern, dressy clothes. Waiter's jacket for Waiter.

Setting: Cozy French restaurant. Table, vase with rose in it, and two chairs are center. Table is set with dinner plates, silverware, etc.

Properties: Tray with coffee cups; menu; handbag with tape recorder.

Lighting: Set may be dimly lit. No special effects.

Raincheck

Characters

GWENDOLYN NABLONSKY, *bank teller*
RICHARD NEVINS, *a bank robber*

TIME: *The present.*
SETTING: *Teller's window at the West Federal Bank. Window is set at an angle so that audience can see both characters. Cash box, papers, pen, and purse are behind counter.*
AT RISE: GWENDOLYN *is standing at window as* RICHARD *enters.*
GWENDOLYN *(Pleasantly):* Next, please. (RICHARD *turns up collar of his jacket, and looking about anxiously, approaches teller's window.* GWENDOLYN *addresses him cheerfully.)* Good morning, sir . . . and welcome to West Federal Bank!
RICHARD *(Glancing to right and left):* Yes—uh—how are you doin'?

GWENDOLYN *(Smiling):* Just fine, sir! And what can we do for you today?

RICHARD *(Clearing his throat and leaning in slightly):* I'd—uh—like to make a withdrawal . . . of a very *large* sum of money.

GWENDOLYN *(Beaming):* Then you've come to the right place—that's what banks are all about!

RICHARD *(Interrupting):* If you don't mind, I'm in kind of a hurry.

GWENDOLYN: Certainly! *(Snaps her fingers)* I'll bet you need money for Christmas shopping!

RICHARD: What?

GWENDOLYN: Christmas shopping. You wouldn't believe all the people who shop early. *(Shrugs)* Of course, it makes sense, the way the stores jack up the prices right after Thanksgiving.

RICHARD *(Impatiently):* Could we just get on with this? *(Clearing throat and looking around nervously)* I—I need one hundred and fifty thousand dollars.

GWENDOLYN: Whatever you say. *(Taking out papers)* Your name, sir?

RICHARD: What?

GWENDOLYN *(Sweetly):* I need your name.

RICHARD: No, you don't.

GWENDOLYN: Sorry—it's bank policy. I need some identification.

RICHARD: Not from *me* you don't.

GWENDOLYN: Are you a celebrity?

RICHARD *(Puzzled):* What?

GWENDOLYN *(With satisfaction):* I thought you looked familiar!

RICHARD *(Looking around; quickly):* No, I don't. You've never seen me before.

GWENDOLYN *(Confused):* You mean you're not someone I'm supposed to know?

RICHARD: Right.

GWENDOLYN *(Firmly):* Then I'm afraid I still need your name.

RICHARD: No, you don't.

GWENDOLYN *(Putting hands on hips):* Do you want me to call the bank manager?

RICHARD *(Quickly):* No. Uh—just put down "John Smith."

GWENDOLYN *(Laughing as she writes):* John Smith? I'll bet you get teased a lot about *that*!

RICHARD *(Seriously):* Not more than once. *(Smiles)* Could I have my money now? O.K.?

GWENDOLYN: Do you have your passbook?

RICHARD: No.

GWENDOLYN: Do you mean you don't have it with you?

RICHARD: I mean I don't have one at all.

GWENDOLYN *(Casually):* Then how about your bank guarantee card?

RICHARD: Nope.

GWENDOLYN: Security Service Approval?

RICHARD: Nope.

GWENDOLYN *(Mystified):* How strange. How long have you been banking with us?

RICHARD: About a minute and a half. *(Pause)* This is my first time in here.

GWENDOLYN: Oh! You're a transfer from another branch! *(Fumbling for papers)* Why didn't you say so?

RICHARD: Because I'm not.

GWENDOLYN: But you *do* have an account with us, don't you?

RICHARD: No.

GWENDOLYN *(Suspiciously):* Then how could you have a hundred fifty thousand dollars in this bank?

RICHARD *(Pleasantly):* I don't.

GWENDOLYN *(Shaking her head):* I'm afraid you've lost me.

RICHARD *(Confidentially):* Do you know what I have in my pocket?

GWENDOLYN *(Irritated):* How am I supposed to know what's in your pocket?

RICHARD *(Matter-of-factly):* I have a grenade . . . capable of blowing up everything on this entire city block.

GWENDOLYN: What! Why are you carrying *that* around?

RICHARD: I'm robbing this bank, and I want one hundred and fifty thousand dollars.

GWENDOLYN *(Uneasily):* You're kidding.

RICHARD: Do I look like a man who kids people?

GWENDOLYN *(Shrugging):* Search me—you're a total stranger to me.

RICHARD *(Explaining):* That's part of my cover—makes the getaway easier.

GWENDOLYN: That's makes sense. *(Pauses)* So John Smith isn't your real name, is it?

RICHARD *(Smiling):* Let's just pretend it is, O.K.? Now, can we get on with this?

GWENDOLYN: Do you do this for a living?

RICHARD: Do what?

GWENDOLYN: Rob banks.

RICHARD *(Annoyed; with sarcasm):* Why don't you say it a little louder? I don't think everyone in the next line heard you.

GWENDOLYN *(Pleasantly):* I said "Rob . . ."

RICHARD: Watch it, lady.

GWENDOLYN: Well, do you do this for a living?

RICHARD: What do you think I am—a stockbroker who got bored during the ten o'clock coffee break?

GWENDOLYN *(Shrugging):* I was just curious.

RICHARD *(Impatiently):* Why don't you just get me the money?

GWENDOLYN: I'm afraid it's not that easy.

RICHARD: Easy? Listen, lady, do you want to trade jobs? It's not that easy for me to stand here and look relaxed, you know.

GWENDOLYN: Are you nervous?

RICHARD *(Quickly; anxiously):* No.

GWENDOLYN: You don't have to get snippy. If you're nervous I understand.

RICHARD: Thanks. Will you just give me the one hundred and fifty thousand?

GWENDOLYN *(Rambling on):* That is a lot of money. I'd be nervous, too. . . . I am *now,* and it's not even my money. *(Sighs; leans forward; confidentially)* Did you know that, according to statistics, a bank is robbed in this city every 4½ minutes?

RICHARD *(Looking at his watch):* Then I'm already late for my next two appointments. Would you hurry up so I won't miss the third?

GWENDOLYN *(Stunned):* You mean you're responsible for all those robberies? I'm really impressed—how do you get away with it?

RICHARD *(Impatiently):* I don't mean to rush you, but it's not supposed to take this long.

GWENDOLYN: It's not easy to get that much money together in a hurry.

RICHARD *(Irritated):* This is a bank, isn't it? You have more money than anyone.

GWENDOLYN: That's certainly true, but a hundred fifty thousand is so *much* money.

RICHARD *(Pointing to her cash box):* How much do you have in there?

GWENDOLYN *(Rummaging through box):* Three hundred twenty.

RICHARD: Then give it to me.

GWENDOLYN *(Puzzled):* Instead of a hundred fifty thousand?

RICHARD: Sure, why not? I can always come back for the balance next week.

GWENDOLYN *(Shrugging):* Suit yourself, but I probably won't be here.

RICHARD: I wasn't serious.

GWENDOLYN: I was. *(Upset)* I'm probably going to lose my job over this.

RICHARD: Over what?

GWENDOLYN: You see, I'm responsible for what's in here. I'm in a lot of trouble if I can't account for every cent at the end of the day.

RICHARD: But being robbed is hardly your fault. Can't you tell them that?

GWENDOLYN: I'm not sure they'd be very understanding. This is my first week here. Don't you think it'd look weird if the bank gets robbed my first week on the job?

RICHARD: Pure coincidence.

GWENDOLYN: Banks just don't see things that way. *(Suddenly)* Tell you what—why don't you get in line again and wait for Bernice's window to open up?

RICHARD: Which one is Bernice?

GWENDOLYN *(Pointing):* Three windows over. She's had a lot more experience with this sort of thing than I have.

RICHARD *(Protesting):* I'm not looking for experience. I'm looking for *money.* A hundred fifty thousand.

GWENDOLYN *(Shaking her head):* That's an awful lot. What are you going to do with it?

RICHARD *(Smiling):* I'm behind with the payments on my yacht. *(Quickly)* Now, do I get my money or not?

GWENDOLYN *(Impressed):* I'll say one thing for you—at least you're keeping your sense of humor.

RICHARD: Which is more than I can say for my patience. *(Looks at his watch)*

GWENDOLYN: Do you know whom you remind me of?

RICHARD *(Bluntly):* No.

GWENDOLYN *(Playfully):* Come on—take a guess.

RICHARD: No. . . . If it's not Robert Redford, I'll be disappointed.

GWENDOLYN: You've even got the same smile.

RICHARD: As who?

GWENDOLYN: It's on the tip of my tongue. Give me a minute to think of it.

RICHARD: Why don't you think of it after I leave?

GWENDOLYN: I've got it! *(Proudly)* Richard Nevins! He sat behind me in homeroom.

RICHARD *(Shaking his head):* That's not who I am.

GWENDOLYN: I didn't say you were; I only said you reminded me of him. *(Continuing)* It is a strange coincidence—you're practically his double.

RICHARD *(Casually):* They say that everyone has one.

GWENDOLYN: Scary, isn't it? Knowing that everyone has someone walking around who looks just like him?

RICHARD: I suppose so. Listen, Miss—

GWENDOLYN *(Holding out her hand to shake his)*: Nablonsky.

RICHARD: What?

GWENDOLYN: That's my name—Gwendolyn Nablonsky.

RICHARD *(Awkwardly)*: Nice to meet you.

GWENDOLYN: Do I look familiar?

RICHARD *(Abruptly)*: No.

GWENDOLYN: I just thought since you looked familiar to me, maybe I looked familiar to you. *(Pauses)* Where did you go to high school?

RICHARD *(Annoyed)*: This is a robbery, remember? Not a reunion.

GWENDOLYN *(Pleased with herself)*: I went to Roosevelt High. Class of '82.

RICHARD: Congratulations.

GWENDOLYN: I just can't get over the resemblance.

RICHARD: Why don't you try? In the meantime, I'll take what's in the cash box.

GWENDOLYN *(Shaking her head)*: Richard would never try something stupid like this.

RICHARD *(Defensively)*: Why not?

GWENDOLYN: Well, why would someone like Richard rob a bank . . . much less threaten to blow it up?

RICHARD: Maybe he fell on hard times.

GWENDOLYN *(Laughing)*: Not likely.

RICHARD: Why not?

GWENDOLYN: Well, because that just doesn't happen to someone voted "Most Likely to Succeed."

RICHARD: So what happened to this guy?

GWENDOLYN: Last thing I heard, he was a cameraman at Paramount. Pretty exciting, huh?

RICHARD *(Rubbing his chin):* Could be—except for all those layoffs.

GWENDOLYN: Oh?

RICHARD *(Continuing):* Yeah, I read about it in the papers. Studio went by seniority—laid off a bunch of guys.

GWENDOLYN *(Nodding):* It is a tough business. That's where my brother works. Hector Nablonsky?

RICHARD *(Intrigued):* Paramount?

GWENDOLYN *(Shaking her head):* Universal. He's in charge of hiring. He's interviewing this week.

RICHARD *(Interested):* Is that so?

GWENDOLYN: He's hiring lots of people. *(Lifts cash box and starts taking out money)* Location work for a new movie . . .

RICHARD *(Indicating cash box):* What are you doing?

GWENDOLYN: I'm getting your money. *(Starts to hand it to him)*

RICHARD *(Pushing it back):* Wait a minute. Let's not rush this.

GWENDOLYN *(Confused):* I thought you were in a hurry.

RICHARD: Yes, but it would be rude to run off while you were in the middle of saying something.

GWENDOLYN: I was finished.

RICHARD: No, you weren't. I interrupted you. You were saying something about a movie.

GWENDOLYN: My brother's hiring some extra people to go on location. *(Offers him money box again)* Do you want this or not? *(He hesitates, then takes the money.)*

RICHARD *(Awkwardly):* It's my first robbery.

GWENDOLYN *(Sympathizing):* I understand.

RICHARD *(Putting money back on counter):* What if we just forget this whole thing? What if I just skip the first time altogether and go straight?

GWENDOLYN: What for?

RICHARD: Because . . . I'm going to give my life a second chance.

GWENDOLYN *(Puzzled):* What if it doesn't work out—the second chance, I mean.

RICHARD: Then I'll come back in a couple days and try again. Keep the money. It's not that important.

GWENDOLYN *(Putting money away):* I wish you'd make up your mind.

RICHARD: It's made up. My life of crime is over.

GWENDOLYN *(Smiling):* That's good. *(Pauses)* Anything else I can do for you today?

RICHARD *(Hesitantly):* Say, could I borrow a dime? *(Shrugs)* I . . . have to make a phone call. (GWEN-DOLYN *takes purse from behind counter and begins rummaging in it. She hands him a coin.*)

GWENDOLYN: Consider it a loan.

RICHARD: Thanks! *(Starts to leave)*

GWENDOLYN: Aren't you forgetting something?

RICHARD: What?

GWENDOLYN: The grenade in your pocket. (RICHARD *grins, reaches into pocket and withdraws an apple. He sets it on the counter.* GWENDOLYN *picks it up.*) Good luck with your new life! *(As* RICHARD *starts to exit, he turns and looks back at her.)*

RICHARD: Nice talking to you. *(Waves and exits)*

GWENDOLYN *(Waving):* 'Bye . . . *(Tosses apple in air and catches it)* Richard. *(Quick curtain)*

THE END

PRODUCTION NOTES

RAINCHECK

Characters: 1 male; 1 female.

Playing Time: 20 minutes.

Costumes: Everyday, modern dress. Richard has apple in jacket pocket.

Properties: Coin; paper money.

Setting: Teller's window at the West Federal Bank. Window is set at an angle so that audience can see both characters. Cash box, papers, pen, and purse are behind counter.

Lighting and Sound: No special effects.

The Knight of the Honest Heart

Characters

SIR CRISPIN, *a young knight*
LADY ELAINE, *a young woman*

TIME: *The Middle Ages.*
SETTING: *A forest somewhere in the heart of England. Rock is down right.*
AT RISE: SIR CRISPIN *is leaning against rock, daydreaming and absently polishing his shield.*
SIR CRISPIN *(Indignantly; putting one hand on his hip and addressing his image in shield):* A fine example of knighthood are you, Sir Crispin! How dare you incur the wrath of the King by even thinking romantically of Lady Elaine! *(Wistfully)* Yet, the most fleeting of seconds in her company is well worth the risk. *(Sighs)* She is beautiful—

she is angelic—*(Shrugs; disappointedly)* she is pledged to another. *(Shaking his head)* What a dilemma! (LADY ELAINE *enters, looking for* SIR CRISPIN.)

LADY ELAINE: Sir Crispin, a word with you. (SIR CRISPIN *almost drops his shield, startled, then quickly recovers and bows as she approaches.*)

SIR CRISPIN: Yes, milady?

LADY ELAINE *(Anxiously):* How many days hence to the palace of your king?

SIR CRISPIN: Three, perhaps, four, milady. You appear tired, milady. Did you sleep well? *(Rests shield against rock)*

LADY ELAINE *(Wearily):* As well as one may, in the open fields. *(Sighs)* And slumber last night was especially difficult.

SIR CRISPIN *(With concern):* Perhaps milady's mind is troubled.

LADY ELAINE *(Shaking her head):* I know not what is troubling me, Sir Crispin. *(Pauses)* When first we began our journey, I had no idea that your master's kingdom was so distant.

SIR CRISPIN *(Nodding):* It is, indeed . . . distant as *(Searching for words)*—gold at rainbow's end! *(Reassuringly)* But it's well worth the travel, milady.

LADY ELAINE *(Curiously):* Tell me, Sir Crispin— what is the kingdom like? Vast, I assume.

SIR CRISPIN *(Shaking his head):* No. But, it's not small, either. *(Gesturing)* All the cottages of the kingdom are clustered close to the castle. The days are tranquil, and the nights are clear, for counting the stars.

LADY ELAINE: His Lordship wrote that the weather *(Pauses, as if trying to remember)* . . . was perfect all year! Is that true?

SIR CRISPIN *(Smiling):* His Lordship does exaggerate a trifle, milady. *(Shrugs)* Actually, it rains most of the time.

LADY ELAINE *(Disturbed):* How dreadful! My gowns shall all be ruined and I myself shall constantly look as if I've just swum across a moat!

SIR CRISPIN *(Quickly):* You would look lovely regardless! *(Embarrassed)* I meant, of course, that when it rains, you will be in the palace.

LADY ELAINE *(Brightening):* Why, of course—in the palace. Tell me about the palace, Sir Crispin, where I am to live as the King's wife.

SIR CRISPIN *(Walking away; embarrassed):* I must confess, milady—I've never been there.

LADY ELAINE *(Alarmed):* But, Sir Crispin—you're a knight. Has the King never invited you to dine there with him and the other knights?

SIR CRISPIN *(Turning):* With other knights, yes, in the Great Hall.

LADY ELAINE: Does the Great Hall have tapestries and lions' heads on the walls? And lamps with a thousand candles?

SIR CRISPIN *(Nodding):* Yes—all the usual things one finds in castles. I'm sure the palace will please you, milady. *(Confidingly)* Thought I should give you warning *(She leans toward him.)*—never wander through the palace without a companion.

LADY ELAINE *(Puzzled):* What unusual advice, Sir Crispin. May I ask the reason?

SIR CRISPIN *(Matter-of-factly):* Ghosts, milady. *(She shrieks.)* They're said to live in the castle and grab hapless victims. Would you like to hear about them?

LADY ELAINE: No, no—another subject, if you please, Sir Crispin. *(She sits on stump, left.)* Have you known His Lordship long?

SIR CRISPIN *(Nodding):* All my life, milady. He has been king for as long as I can remember.

LADY ELAINE *(Unhappily):* Then His Lordship must be *(Hesitating)* old.

SIR CRISPIN *(Quickly):* But very wise.

LADY ELAINE *(Pacing nervously):* Is he—a kind person?

SIR CRISPIN *(Smiling):* Very kind. *(In warning tone)* Provided he is not vexed. *(Laughs; reassuringly)* I'm sure everything will be all right—you needn't worry.

LADY ELAINE *(Concerned):* Is His Lordship tall or short?

SIR CRISPIN: Why, he's . . . *(Catches himself)* Let's say—*(Pauses)* Does it matter?

LADY ELAINE *(Frustrated);* No, but I do wonder. May I ask one more question, Sir Crispin?

SIR CRISPIN *(Bowing):* Certainly, milady.

LADY ELAINE: Is His Lordship handsome?

SIR CRISPIN *(Amused):* Milady asks a thousand questions! If you persist in asking, and I answer your every question, you shall have no surprises left for your arrival.

LADY ELAINE *(Stubbornly):* One does have reason to wonder, Sir Crispin, when one receives a proposal of marriage by messenger. Do you not find that odd?

SIR CRISPIN: The King would have come himself, milady, but there are quests to pursue and fierce dragons to conquer. These activities fill the hours of the King's day.

LADY ELAINE *(Nodding):* I understand, of course, that there are matters of state to which he must give his attention. *(Studying* SIR CRISPIN*)* How loyal you must be, for the King to entrust you with my safety.

SIR CRISPIN *(Uneasily):* I try to serve His Lordship faithfully.

LADY ELAINE: Have you a family, Sir Crispin?

SIR CRISPIN *(Nodding):* An aged mother . . . and six brothers.

LADY ELAINE: Are your brothers knights, as well?

SIR CRISPIN: No, only I am a knight.

LADY ELAINE: And—have you a sweetheart?

SIR CRISPIN *(Flustered):* No, milady—just being a knight keeps me occupied. *(Abruptly)* But I didn't finish telling you about the kingdom.

LADY ELAINE: Yes, do go on.

SIR CRISPIN: There's . . . *(Pondering what to say; then suddenly)* a large moat about the castle. You can only get into the castle over a drawbridge. And the moat is filled with ducks. *(Pauses for suspense)*

LADY ELAINE *(Amazed):* Live ducks?

SIR CRISPIN: Of course! You can feed them!

LADY ELAINE: I've never fed ducks before. It would be fun. May I feed them every day?

SIR CRISPIN *(Laughing):* The bride of the King shouldn't spend all her time feeding ducks. *(She turns away, hurt)* Wait! I suppose there'd be no harm in it. Of course, you'll probably have to drop the food from your window—I doubt if the King would want you to run about outside the castle, because of bandits.

LADY ELAINE *(Alarmed):* I didn't know there were bandits.

SIR CRISPIN: Yes, they lurk in the woods near the castle.

LADY ELAINE *(Disappointed):* Shall I have to stay within the castle walls the rest of my life, then?

SIR CRISPIN: Yes, but you'll have embroidery and music.

LADY ELAINE *(Sadly):* I see.

SIR CRISPIN *(Continuing):* Sometimes we have bonfires and carnivals—*(Excitedly)* I once saw a dancing bear, and a juggler who could swallow fire! *(More seriously)* Of course, you must attend palace functions. Many such events take place.

LADY ELAINE *(Hopefully):* Will I see you there?

SIR CRISPIN *(Shaking his head):* No. That would be strictly for royalty. *(Pauses)* But you'll see the King's mother.

LADY ELAINE: Will I like her?

SIR CRISPIN: I wouldn't place a wager on it. *(Confidingly)* I hope you won't mention this to the King, but his mother is rather domineering. *(Shrugs)* But you'll get used to her in time, I'm sure.

LADY ELAINE: *Your* mother—what is *she* like?

SIR CRISPIN *(Perplexed):* What an odd question, milady.

LADY ELAINE: The journey has been so long, Sir Crispin—I yearn to hear of other people's lives.

SIR CRISPIN: Very well, then. She bakes the most delicious honey cakes in all the land.

LADY ELAINE *(Reflecting):* That sweet morsel we enjoyed at midday—was that such a honey cake?

SIR CRISPIN: It was, indeed.

LADY ELAINE: Absolutely divine! And will I partake of such desserts in the palace?

SIR CRISPIN: I fear not, milady, for the King is not partial to such things.

LADY ELAINE *(Disappointedly):* With such sparse fare, at least I shall not outgrow my dresses— that's the bright side, is it not?

SIR CRISPIN: Not quite so bright, milady. The palace tasters sample everything on His Lordship's plate—and yours, too. I hear that the appetites of the official tasters are voracious, and that they consider a meal not well sampled until they have eaten *half* of it.

LADY ELAINE: Why on earth would the King have tasters to sample his meals?

SIR CRISPIN: He is worried about being poisoned, milady.

LADY ELAINE *(Upset):* You mean that I shall never get to eat an entire apple?

SIR CRISPIN: I'm afraid not, milady. And more's the pity, for the finest fruit anywhere grows in our valley. *(She rises and paces.)* Does something trouble you, milady?

LADY ELAINE *(Sadly):* Why, Sir Crispin, it seems that all the pleasures of your kingdom are reserved for the poor.

SIR CRISPIN: Sometimes, the simplest pleasures are the best, milady.

LADY ELAINE *(Unhappily):* I'll have a dreadful time, living in the palace, shut away.

SIR CRISPIN *(Comfortingly):* It won't be as bad as you think, milady. I may have exaggerated a trifle.

LADY ELAINE *(Moving toward him):* Sir Crispin, are you not called the Knight of the Honest Heart?

SIR CRISPIN: I am, milady.

LADY ELAINE: Then may I confide in you?

SIR CRISPIN: Certainly.

LADY ELAINE *(With difficulty; wringing her hands)*: I'm—not Lady Elaine.

SIR CRISPIN *(Astonished)*: You're jesting! *(She shakes her head.)* You're *not* jesting? *(She shakes her head again.)* May I ask, then—who *are* you, if not Lady Elaine?

LADY ELAINE: I'm her lady-in-waiting.

SIR CRISPIN *(Upset)*: I don't understand.

LADY ELAINE: When you arrived at our palace, your message was given to me first—Lady Elaine does not know how to read. And so I did a most terrible thing.

SIR CRISPIN *(Folding his arms)*: I'm ready to listen.

LADY ELAINE: I didn't give Lady Elaine the message. I told her that a relative of mine had been taken ill, and that I had to leave at once. Then I came here with you in her place.

SIR CRISPIN: Forgive me for asking, but why?

LADY ELAINE: I had grown weary of being a lady-in-waiting, Sir Crispin, for all I did was— *(Shrugs)* wait. I so desperately wanted something exciting to happen in my life. You offered that chance. *(Pauses)* I told you that I was Lady Elaine, hoping that you and the King might provide a better life than the one I had known. *(Sadly)* Only I see now that as the bride of the King I shall never be happy again.

SIR CRISPIN *(Worried)*: The King is not going to like this.

LADY ELAINE *(Anxiously):* Perhaps he need not know.

SIR CRISPIN *(Aghast):* I dare not deceive the King!

LADY ELAINE *(Sighing):* I fear you're right, Sir Crispin. But what choice have I now? I cannot continue my masquerade—shall I run away?

SIR CRISPIN: Where would you go? If, indeed, I let you escape?

LADY ELAINE *(Sighing):* Why, back to the real Lady Elaine, I suppose, though I know the time will surely come again when I will want to escape, as I am doing now. *(Sighs)* Lady Elaine is a dreadful bore.

SIR CRISPIN: By the way, need I still address you as milady?

LADY ELAINE *(Smiling):* My name is Celia. Celia the Hopeless.

SIR CRISPIN: I think I can offer you a remedy for your plight.

LADY ELAINE: In what way?

SIR CRISPIN *(Matter-of-factly):* Marry *me*.

LADY ELAINE *(Stunned):* Marry *you*? *(Shakes her head)* Your King will be angered enough to learn that I am of common blood and unworthy of his attention. It's best, I think, that he not be angry with you as well.

SIR CRISPIN: Actually, Celia *(Hesitates)*—the King doesn't even know who I am.

LADY ELAINE *(Puzzled):* I don't understand, Sir Crispin—he dubbed you a knight, didn't he?

SIR CRISPIN *(Nervously):* Would you like me any less if I were just "Crispin" without the "Sir" in front of it?

LADY ELAINE *(Confused):* Aren't you really a knight?

SIR CRISPIN *(Shaking his head; sadly):* Not even a page.

LADY ELAINE: Then . . . what are you?

SIR CRISPIN: My brothers and I are shoemakers.

LADY ELAINE *(Amused):* Now *I* am ready to listen to *you.*

SIR CRISPIN *(Pacing):* I set off on an adventure one day, and lodged for a night in your kingdom. There, I heard of a fair princess who lived in the castle. And the more I heard, the more I yearned to meet her. However brief our encounter, it would be wonderful to share with my brothers when I returned.

LADY ELAINE: But how were you able to enter the palace?

SIR CRISPIN: By becoming the Knight of the Honest Heart.

LADY ELAINE *(Indicating his outfit):* Where did you get your clothes for that deception?

SIR CRISPIN: I spent what money I had for some of them and traded my possessions, too, so that I could present myself in noble attire at your court. *(Correcting himself)* I mean, at the court of Lady Elaine. *(Shrugs)* I never expected that she would believe my story of a distant liege who sought her hand in matrimony. *(Sadly)* And when you accepted . . . I hadn't the courage to tell you I had presented myself under false pretenses. Indeed, it wasn't entirely untrue. The King has been seeking a bride.

LADY ELAINE: But one of noble birth, I vow.

SIR CRISPIN *(Kneeling; ardently):* I shall not ask you to forgive me, though in my heart, I should wish for it a hundred times, milady.

LADY ELAINE *(Touched):* You needn't call me milady. I'm not a princess.

SIR CRISPIN *(Putting his hand on his heart):* In my heart, you are. *(Pauses)* I shall return you to your land at daybreak. *(Rises)*

LADY ELAINE *(Sadly):* Then I shall never see you again, shall I?

SIR CRISPIN: No, milady.

LADY ELAINE *(Starting off, then turning back to him):* Sir Crispin?

SIR CRISPIN: Yes?

LADY ELAINE: The people of your kingdom—do they live happily ever after?

SIR CRISPIN *(Smiling):* Almost all of them.

LADY ELAINE: And do they feed ducks, and attend carnivals, and eat all the honey cakes they desire?

SIR CRISPIN *(Nodding):* That was one of the rare elements of truth in my narration.

LADY: Then, as Lady Elaine, I demand that you deliver me there at once. *(Laughing)* What say you, Crispin?

SIR CRISPIN *(Breaking into a smile and bowing):* I am your obedient servant, Celia. *(Curtain)*

THE END

PRODUCTION NOTES

THE KNIGHT OF THE HONEST HEART

Characters: 1 male; 1 female.

Playing Time: 15 minutes.

Costumes: Sir Crispin wears black, belted tunic with a silver crest on the front, black tights, and boots. Lady Elaine wears a long gown that suggests royalty but is not overly extravagant.

Properties: Sword; shield.

Setting: Forest. Rock, down right. Exit upstage.

Lighting: No special effects.

A Loan for Columbus

Characters

SECRETARY
MR. SANTIAGO
MR. DOMINGO
CHRISTOPHER COLUMBUS

TIME: *1492.*

SETTING: *Mr. Santiago's office at the First Bank of Castille, Spain. Desk is center, with large stuffed chair at either side. Window upstage looks out on city. Door to outer office is right.*

AT RISE: MR. SANTIAGO *and* MR. DOMINGO *are seated, drinking coffee.* DOMINGO *is in the middle of a story.*

DOMINGO: And then I say, "Now, I don't want to *(With emphasis) bore* you, but pork futures are definitely the way to go!" *(Both laugh.)*

SECRETARY *(Entering):* Excuse me, Mr. Santiago,

but your eleven o'clock appointment is here.

SANTIAGO: Thanks. Show him in. (SECRETARY *exits*.)

DOMINGO *(Rising):* Well, I'd better get going.

SANTIAGO *(Stopping him):* On the contrary, I think you may want to stay for this one.

DOMINGO: A new loan applicant?

SANTIAGO: Yes, and the funniest explanation you'll ever hear.

DOMINGO: Oh? What is it?

SANTIAGO: I'll let him explain. *(Snickering)* I don't think I could tell you with a straight face. (SECRETARY *and* CHRISTOPHER COLUMBUS *enter.*) Ah— here he is now.

SECRETARY: Our loan officer, Mr. Santiago. (CHRISTOPHER *crosses to shake his hand.*) This is Christopher Columbus, sir. (SECRETARY *exits.*)

SANTIAGO: How do you do, Mr. Columbus? *(Introducing* DOMINGO) This is Mr. Domingo, one of our vice presidents. (CHRISTOPHER *and* DOMINGO *shake hands.*) So, what brings you to Castille, Mr. Columbus?

CHRISTOPHER: I'm here for a loan, sir. A modest sum, you might say, to tide me over.

DOMINGO: Tide you over?

CHRISTOPHER: Yes . . . over the ocean. I'm planning to make a trip.

DOMINGO: Ah, yes—a vacation loan, is it?

CHRISTOPHER: No. I'd say it's strictly business.

DOMINGO: When were you planning to leave?

CHRISTOPHER: As soon as possible. I have the ships picked out already.

SANTIAGO: Ships? More than one?

CHRISTOPHER: Yes, sir. Three of them.

DOMINGO *(Suppressing a chuckle):* You must have a lot of luggage to need three ships.

CHRISTOPHER: Actually, I'm packing very light. I'm just planning to bring a lot back with me.

SANTIAGO: It is hard to resist those tourist traps.

DOMINGO: And where are you planning to go with your three ships, Mr. Columbus?

CHRISTOPHER *(Dramatically):* I'm sailing west to the Indies!

DOMINGO: Indies, did you say?

CHRISTOPHER: Yes, the Indies.

DOMINGO *(Slowly):* I don't believe I've ever heard of the Indies.

CHRISTOPHER: Of course not. That's because I'll be the first person ever to go there.

SANTIAGO *(A bit sarcastically):* And where is this place, Mr. Columbus?

CHRISTOPHER *(Hesistantly):* That's a little hard to explain.

SANTIAGO: Well, I'm afraid that banks deal in exact information. If you'd like the First Bank of Castille to finance such a junket for you, we do want a precise plan.

CHRISTOPHER: Let me put it this way: Do you know how—when you stand on a beach and look way out to sea—everything seems to end at the horizon?

DOMINGO: Of course. What about it?

CHRISTOPHER: My theory, sir, is that it doesn't.

DOMINGO: Does what?

CHRISTOPHER: Come to an end. I think there's a whole world over the horizon waiting for someone to discover it. *(Firmly)* And I plan to be that someone.

DOMINGO *(Wryly):* With money from the First Bank of Castille?

CHRISTOPHER: I certainly hope so.

SANTIAGO: Mr. Columbus, do you read the papers?

CHRISTOPHER: Every morning. Why do you ask?

SANTIAGO: Then surely you've read commentaries by the best scientists in our country who state most assuredly that the world is flat as a tortilla. What you see at the end of the horizon, quite clearly, is all there is.

CHRISTOPHER *(Protesting):* But how do they know? Have they ever taken a ship and sailed out as far as they could go?

SANTIAGO *(Impatiently):* Of course they have. And just before they got to the edge, they were smart enough to turn around and come home before they fell off.

DOMINGO: In a nutshell, Mr. Columbus, he's trying to say that eyebrows would indeed be raised in financial circles if the First Bank of Castille were to provide funds for ventures as ridiculous as the one you've just proposed.

CHRISTOPHER *(Looking off; dramatically):* I could

be blazing a trail for millions.

SANTIAGO: But think of the cost, Mr. Columbus . . .

CHRISTOPHER *(With a wave of his word):* A small price to pay for adventure. Why, I can get the *Nina, Pinta,* and *Santa Maria* for only—

DOMINGO: Pardon me, but who are they?

CHRISTOPHER: Those are the names of the three ships. I can outfit all three for a little less than five thousand dollars.

SANTIAGO: Mr. Columbus, five thousand is a considerable sum, especially considering that we have no guarantee you'll be able to pay us back, or for that matter, come back yourself.

CHRISTOPHER: Of course I will!

SANTIAGO *(Picking up application and scanning it):* According to your application, Mr. Columbus, you haven't mentioned any collateral.

CHRISTOPHER: Well . . .

DOMINGO *(Looking at him closely):* You *do* have collateral, don't you?

CHRISTOPHER: Uh . . . how much collateral would you consider appropriate?

SANTIAGO: Well, in cases like this, where a high risk is involved, I'd say that ten thousand would be fair.

CHRISTOPHER: If I had ten thousand, why would I come to a bank for five?

DOMINGO *(Trying to be patient):* Do you have investments, then?

CHRISTOPHER: I invest everything in dreams, sir.

SANTIAGO *(Sarcastically):* Yes, but dreams don't

pay the rent, do they, Mr. Columbus?

CHRISTOPHER *(Urgently):* But this dream is going to pay off, I can just feel it in my bones. . . .

DOMINGO: We admire your conviction, Mr. Columbus, but we hold a position of public trust. You seem to be an ambitious young man who's probably going places.

SANTIAGO *(Blandly):* Unfortunately, the Indies isn't one of them—at least not with backing from the First Bank of Castille.

CHRISTOPHER *(Loudly):* But you're closing your eyes to incredible opportunity.

DOMINGO: No, sir, we're simply trying to open your eyes to dangers that you're clearly not aware of.

CHRISTOPHER *(Impatiently):* Dangers? What kind of dangers?

SANTIAGO: Have you stopped to consider what would happen if you sailed too far—over the edge?

DOMINGO: Huge, scaly monsters with yellow eyes and long tails and claws the size of a house would reach out and grab you as soon as your boat teetered precariously on the brink. And your sails would catch fire from their hot breath.

SANTIAGO *(Dramatically):* And in a single crunch of their fangs, you'd be gone forever!

CHRISTOPHER *(Excitedly):* No, no! That's not the way it is at all!

SANTIAGO: But of course it is!

DOMINGO: You sail to the edge and, in a flash, it's all over. Pffft. End of voyage.

SANTIAGO: And no repayment of the loan.

DOMINGO: I'm sure you can understand our position.

CHRISTOPHER *(Sighing):* If only you'd try to see it my way, just once. You sail for weeks at a time on a shimmering blue-green sea. And then, all of a sudden, rising like a giant out of the water, you see it—land! And as you get closer, you see spacious skies and purple mountains and amber fields of grain. And maybe—if I'm not mistaken—

SANTIAGO: Yes?

CHRISTOPHER: People. People very much like us. Why, they probably even have banks just like this one. Only instead of the Bank of Castille it's probably called Bank of the Indies. Who knows? Maybe even as we speak, there's someone just like me sitting in an office just like this and asking for a loan to come and see if there's anything on this side of the ocean.

DOMINGO *(Sarcastically):* Well, after he makes a safe crossing, Mr. Columbus, we'd be happy to reconsider a reciprocal voyage. *(Shrugs)* In the meantime, though—

CHRISTOPHER: You're saying no, then?

SANTIAGO: It's for your own good, of course. We wouldn't want anything to happen to you.

DOMINGO: Or to our money. (SECRETARY *enters.*)

SECRETARY: Excuse me, Mr. Santiago, but your lunch date is here.

SANTIAGO *(Groaning):* Oh, no! I forgot all about her.

DOMINGO: Who?

SANTIAGO: Queen Isabella. And I've already made

other plans. How could I be so stupid?

DOMINGO *(Shaking his head):* She'll be upset if you turn her down.

SANTIAGO *(Sighing):* Don't I know it? Domingo, could you take my place?

DOMINGO *(Shaking his head):* Sorry. I have a Board meeting.

SANTIAGO: But I can't just leave her without a luncheon companion.

CHRISTOPHER *(Preparing to exit):* Well, if no is your final answer to my request—*(Picking up his hat)*

SANTIAGO *(Suddenly):* Wait a minute! I just thought of something!

DOMINGO *(Curiously):* What is it?

SANTIAGO *(To* CHRISTOPHER*):* Are you doing anything for lunch, Mr. Columbus?

CHRISTOPHER: Oh, I thought I'd grab a bite in the plaza.

SANTIAGO *(Casually):* How would you like to have lunch with Queen Isabella?

CHRISTOPHER: Why would I want to have lunch with her?

SANTIAGO: Well, because she's always interested in bright and amusing conversation—I'm sure she'd be delighted with you.

CHRISTOPHER: Well . . . I suppose . . .

SANTIAGO: As a favor to us, Mr. Columbus?

CHRISTOPHER *(Suspiciously):* A favor you plan to return?

DOMINGO *(Quickly):* Of course! *(After a pause)*

Would reconsideration of your loan papers be enough?

CHRISTOPHER *(Excitedly):* Would it!

SANTIAGO *(Hastily):* We'd have to get back to you, naturally. These things take time.

CHRISTOPHER *(Sighing):* Well, it's worth a chance.

SANTIAGO *(To* SECRETARY): Let Her Majesty know that Mr. Columbus will be right out to accompany her to lunch. (SECRETARY *nods and exits.*)

CHRISTOPHER: But what do I say? What shall we talk about?

DOMINGO *(Leading* CHRISTOPHER *to door):* I'm sure you'll think of something.

CHRISTOHER *(Inspired):* I could tell her about my voyage!

SANTIAGO *(Agreeably):* Just the thing! She'll find it all most fascinating, I'm sure.

CHRISTOPHER *(At door):* You won't forget, will you? About reviewing my application?

DOMINGO: It will be our number one priority. *(Lets him out and closes door)*

SANTIAGO *(Smiling):* You can't be serious, Domingo.

DOMINGO *(Strolling back to desk):* It got you off the hook, didn't it?

SANTIAGO: But we'll be the laughing stock of the Board if we present this application to them.

DOMINGO *(Picking up application):* But that's the point.

SANTIAGO: What is?

DOMINGO *(Tearing up application):* We won't.

SANTIAGO *(Laughing, then suddenly stopping):* That really wasn't a very nice thing to do.

DOMINGO *(With a wave of his hand):* No harm done. The Queen will listen politely to his story, they'll finish their lunch, and that will be the end of it.

SANTIAGO *(Laughing again):* Change the course of history, indeed! Discover new worlds! *(Shakes his head)*

DOMINGO: We really did do him a big favor, you know.

SANTIAGO: Yes, but then that's what we're here for.

DOMINGO: To lend a hand.

SANTIAGO: And sometimes, even lend money.

DOMINGO: True. But only for good causes. For things that are down-to-earth.

SANTIAGO *(Laughing):* Instead of off the edge of it! *(Quick curtain)*

THE END

PRODUCTION NOTES

A LOAN FOR COLUMBUS

Characters: 3 male; 1 female.

Playing Time: 15 minutes.

Costumes: All wear costumes of the period.

Properties: Coffee cups; application.

Setting: Mr. Santiago's office at the First Bank of Castille, Spain. Desk is center, with large stuffed chair at either side. Window upstage looks out on city. Door to outer office is right.

Lighting and Sound: No special effects.

Desperately Seeking Princess

Characters

FREDDIE
CINDY
JAMES

TIME: *The present, a Saturday evening.*
SETTING: *Split set. Freddie's elegant hotel room in downtown San Francisco is at right. A telephone and a vase of fresh roses are on coffee table, which has two chairs behind it. There is a stereo at far right. At left is Cindy's modest apartment. There is a single chair, and a small table with telephone and teacup on it. On a larger table to left stand a potted plant, watering can, hairbrush and nail file.*
AT RISE: FREDDIE *enters right, carrying a grocery bag. He turns on stereo; classical music is heard.*

He takes bag of potato chips and a soda from grocery bag and starts to eat chips. After a moment, CINDY, *casually dressed, enters carrying newspaper. She scans classified section, ponders the ads. After a pause, she crosses to phone, and checks number in the ad again before dialing. The phone rings in* FREDDIE'S *room, and he crosses to answer it.*

FREDDIE *(Into phone):* Hello?

CINDY *(Brightly):* Hi. I'm calling about the ad in the paper.

FREDDIE: Could you be more specific? I don't want you to be disappointed.

CINDY: About what?

FREDDIE *(Jokingly):* Well, how do I know you're not calling about a '59 Buick, or a washer and dryer?

CINDY: I'm not.

FREDDIE *(Smiling):* Good. Neither one of those is in my ad.

CINDY *(Gathering her courage):* I'm calling about the one in the "Personals" column. "Bewitched Frog Seeks Princess."

FREDDIE *(Pleased):* That's me.

CINDY *(Skeptically):* You're the Bewitched Frog? *(Sets paper down on table)*

FREDDIE *(Nodding as he takes sip of soda):* Uh-huh. Are you a princess?

CINDY *(Smiling):* Not exactly.

FREDDIE *(Disappointed):* Oh. What are you?

CINDY *(Matter-of-factly):* I'm a typist. I work for the state.

FREDDIE: Then you're not from royalty?

CINDY *(Shaking her head):* Hinkley.

FREDDIE *(Puzzled):* I beg your pardon?

CINDY: Hinkley, Ohio—that's where I'm from.

FREDDIE *(Irritated):* If you're not a princess, why are you calling?

CINDY *(Shrugging):* Curiosity—to see what kind of person would put that kind of ad in the paper.

FREDDIE *(Annoyed):* Well, now that you know, there's little more to say. *(Starts to hang up)*

CINDY *(Quickly):* Wait! Don't hang up!

FREDDIE *(Putting phone back to ear):* Did you saying something?

CINDY: Well, what do you want me to say?

FREDDIE *(Smiling):* I really don't know you well enough to offer any suggestions.

CINDY *(Laughing):* You don't know me at all!

FREDDIE: Well then, who are you? What's your name?

CINDY *(Stiffly):* I'd rather not say.

FREDDIE *(Amused):* A woman of mystery, hm-m?

CINDY *(Emphatically):* I don't give my name to strange men.

FREDDIE: You mean you just call them up anonymously?

CINDY *(Indignantly):* For your information, I've never done this before in my life!

FREDDIE *(Sipping soda):* Why are you doing it now?

CINDY *(Shrugging):* I told you before—curiosity.

FREDDIE *(Impatiently):* We seem to be going

around in a circle. Isn't this where I say goodbye and hang up?

CINDY *(At a loss for words):* Well . . .

FREDDIE *(Crisply):* Nice talking to you. *(Starts to hang up)*

CINDY *(Quickly):* Wait!

FREDDIE: Yes?

CINDY: I thought of something to say.

FREDDIE *(In mock amazement):* We're making progress! What is it you have to say?

CINDY *(Awkwardly):* Have you had many calls . . . about your ad?

FREDDIE: Why do you ask?

CINDY: It's just sort of unusual . . . as if it were a code or something.

FREDDIE: Would you be flattered if I told you you're the first one?

CINDY: Am I?

FREDDIE: That's not the question—the question is whether you'd be flattered if you *were*.

CINDY *(Sitting):* Sure—I guess so.

FREDDIE: All right . . . you're the very first one. Congratulations.

CINDY *(Nonplussed):* Oh.

FREDDIE *(With pleasant sarcasm):* You disguise your enthusiasm well.

CINDY: Well, I don't know whether I should be flattered or not. You have to admit it's a pretty bizarre ad.

FREDDIE: Do you think so?

CINDY: It's cute . . . but still bizarre.

FREDDIE: You answered it, didn't you?

CINDY *(Insistently):* But don't you think it's a demeaning way to meet people?

FREDDIE *(Pulling up chair to sit down):* I never said anything about *meeting* anyone. What's wrong with just talking on the phone?

CINDY: Because eventually it will lead to meeting you . . . and then falling in love and out of love and being depressed . . .

FREDDIE *(Nodding gravely):* Sounds serious. Maybe we should hang up now.

CINDY: No, not yet. Tell me why you're doing this— advertising yourself in the classifieds . . . like a garage sale?

FREDDIE *(Humoring her):* Because I'm a great bargain—witty, wonderful, dynamic—

CINDY *(Firmly):* Be serious.

FREDDIE: If I give you a straight answer will you tell me why you called? *(Sips soda)*

CINDY: I already did. *(Sips tea)*

FREDDIE: Not good enough. Lurking behind that pretty head of yours is an ulterior motive.

CINDY *(Momentarily flattered):* How did you know I'm pretty?

FREDDIE: So, I'm right?

CINDY *(Coyly):* Of course. But how did you know?

FREDDIE: You have a nice voice. I'm only guessing the rest.

CINDY: Thanks.

FREDDIE *(Continuing):* Clearly not the kind of voice that belongs in a 300-pound, redheaded, stand-in for the Bride of Frankenstein.

CINDY: You're very perceptive.

FREDDIE: Thank you. *(Sips soda)*

CINDY: What else do you perceive?

FREDDIE *(Thinking a moment):* Blonde?

CINDY *(Shaking head):* Brunette.

FREDDIE: Tall?

CINDY *(Shaking head):* Wrong again.

FREDDIE: I'd better quit. What do you think of me?

CINDY *(Smiling);* You have a very nice voice.

FREDDIE: Flatterer.

CINDY *(Curiously):* What do *you* look like? *(Strolls to plant table)*

FREDDIE *(Slyly):* Ah—you're intrigued?

CINDY *(Casually):* Slightly. *(Absently, picks up brush from table and brushes hair)*

FREDDIE: O.K. I'm five-foot-four, balding, overweight. I have yellow fangs, and at night I hang by my heels from the shower rod.

CINDY *(Amused):* You're kidding.

FREDDIE: Why would I be kidding? *(Pause)* All right, you caught me. I threw in a couple of extra details for color. Are you still intrigued?

CINDY *(Drily):* At least you're honest. Most people who do things like this would say they're tall, dark, and handsome.

FREDDIE *(Melodramatically):* Really? What cads!

CINDY *(Sipping tea):* Of course, since the chances of

our meeting are extremely remote, it really doesn't matter, does it?

FREDDIE: In that case, I'm Superman's twin brother.

CINDY (*Raising eyebrows*): Oh?

FREDDIE: Yes. We're frequently mistaken for one another.

CINDY (*Sarcastically*): I liked you a lot better when you were five-foot-four and humble.

FREDDIE: I'll take that as a compliment.

CINDY: You still haven't told me why you did it.

FREDDIE: I feel as if I'm on trial here. Are you always this inquisitive?

CINDY: Constantly. Are you always this evasive?

FREDDIE: Shall I plead self-defense or insanity?

CINDY: The latter seems more appropriate. (*Jokingly*) Don't you have to get back to your room before they discover you're missing?

FREDDIE (*Confidently*): I bribed the guards. (*Pause*) Do you really want to know why I placed the ad?

CINDY (*Crossing to chair with phone; sitting*): Yes.

FREDDIE: To talk to someone who'd accept me without knowing what I am.

CINDY (*Curiously*): Why? What are you? (*Laughs*) No, wait—don't tell me—a frog, right? (*Puts phone on table*)

FREDDIE: You could say that. Not your regular garden variety, mind you. A bewitched frog. There's a difference.

CINDY: Do you mean that you're really a prince?

FREDDIE: Actually only a Count—a few ranks below a prince.

CINDY *(Mockingly):* That's false advertising. You could get in trouble.

FREDDIE *(Seriously):* But it caught your attention.

CINDY *(Suspiciously):* Is this some kind of fraternity initiation? Am I being taped?

FREDDIE: No—I'm on the level.

CINDY: Well, I do have to give you credit for originality.

FREDDIE *(Pleased):* Is that what made you select me?

CINDY *(Indignantly):* I beg your pardon. I haven't selected you for anything.

FREDDIE: You selected my ad.

CINDY: Only after a toss-up.

FREDDIE: Who was the competition?

CINDY *(Picking up the paper and reading):* "Chubby but sincere backpacker seeks female companion to share romance and expenses of trek to Point Barrow, Alaska."

FREDDIE *(Nodding):* Sounds as if he has potential. Anybody else?

CINDY *(Reading):* "Suave, rich businessman seeks shapely young protégée for discreet luncheons and intellectual repartee." *(To* FREDDIE) What do you think?

FREDDIE *(Mysteriously):* Maybe I'm the same guy. *(Shrugs)* I could have two different phone numbers to throw you off, you know.

CINDY: That's not true—is it?

FREDDIE: Actually . . . no.

CINDY: Why do you have such a problem meeting people that you have to place ads in the *Chronicle*?

FREDDIE: I don't. It's meeting people I like that's the problem.

CINDY: Where have you been looking?

FREDDIE: Obviously in all the wrong places . . . or I would have met you. *(Shrugs)* Instead I meet *them*.

CINDY: Who?

FREDDIE: "Marriageable young women." Everywhere I go, there they are—veritable swarms.

CINDY *(Sarcastically)*: Maybe it's your after-shave lotion.

FREDDIE *(Exasperated)*: Has anyone ever told you that you have a very weird sense of humor?

CINDY *(Sipping tea)*: Only my boyfriend.

FREDDIE *(Caught off guard)*: You didn't tell me you have a boyfriend.

CINDY: It's O.K. He's been gone now for some time.

FREDDIE: For the evening . . . or permanently?

CINDY: Quite permanently, as a matter of fact.

FREDDIE: Oh, I'm sorry.

CINDY: That's all right.

FREDDIE *(Concerned)*: When did he pass on?

CINDY *(Laughing)*: I didn't mean gone as in dead; I meant gone as in years ago. High school. We broke up and he married my best friend, Thelma. I must have cried for at least a week and a half.

FREDDIE: That's too bad.

CINDY: On the contrary—it's great! I don't have to worry about calls at 3 A.M. to borrow my math homework.

FREDDIE *(Sipping):* What does he do now?

CINDY: Search me—that guy had absolutely no talent.

FREDDIE: How about you?

CINDY: Me? *(Coyly)* I'm loaded with talent.

FREDDIE: What I really meant was, do you have a hard time meeting people, too?

CINDY: Oh. Not really. I have a roommate who considers herself the matchmaker of the century. *(Suddenly)* Hey—maybe she could fix you up!

FREDDIE: Great! How about with her roommate?

CINDY *(Surprised):* Me?

FREDDIE: Why not?

CINDY *(Shaking her head):* I told you before that it's not going to work out.

FREDDIE: Give it a chance. How about tomorrow? Do you like pizza?

CINDY: What's the rush?

FREDDIE: Would you like to go or not?

CINDY: I don't like being rushed for no reason.

FREDDIE: Actually . . . there is a reason.

CINDY: What?

FREDDIE: It's my uncle . . . my favorite uncle.

CINDY: You're trying to fix me up with your uncle?

FREDDIE: No, of course not.

CINDY: Then what does he have to do with anything?

FREDDIE *(Quietly):* He's very ill. I owe him a lot.

CINDY: I'm sorry he's ill. But what do you owe him?

FREDDIE: To be perfectly honest, he'd like to see me settle down and get married.

CINDY: Why don't you?

FREDDIE: I haven't met the right person. For that matter, I haven't had a chance to meet the right one, to let her get to know me for myself. I want to have the time to find out what she likes, tell her what I like—

CINDY: What do you like?

FREDDIE *(Reflectively):* I like New York in June. . . . a fireside when a storm is due . . .

CINDY: If you throw in "potato chips and moonlight cruises," I think we've got the makings of a song.

FREDDIE: How about you?

CINDY *(Shrugging):* Glamour, glitter—all the jet-set stuff.

FREDDIE *(Pleased):* We're perfect—they say opposites attract. Is tomorrow night O.K.?

CINDY: You're really serious about this, aren't you?

FREDDIE: Yes! Aren't you?

CINDY: I don't even know you!

FREDDIE: I'll introduce myself at 7:00. May I pick you up?

CINDY: You don't know where I live.

FREDDIE: You could tell me.

CINDY: Yes, I could. Or I could pick you up.

FREDDIE *(Amused):* Because you're a liberated woman?

CINDY: No . . . because I'm not ready for you to know where I live.

FREDDIE: Why don't we compromise? There's a restaurant down the street with these big yellow arches—you can't miss 'em.

CINDY: Good grief! First you tell me you're a Count, then you invite me out for a hamburger. This is ridiculous.

FREDDIE: Simple pleasures, milady. If I ever become king, I won't be able to do such things.

CINDY *(Skeptically):* Oh, really? Are you in line for the job?

FREDDIE: Yes, but I'd rather be in line for a chocolate shake and fries. I intend to sweep you off your feet.

CINDY: Ah, happily ever-after fairy tale!

FREDDIE *(Concerned):* Why do I get the impression you're getting the wrong impression?

CINDY *(Impatiently):* Listen, this whole thing is getting out of hand—why don't we put a stop to it before we're both sorry?

FREDDIE *(Urgently):* No, please. I'd really like to meet you. (JAMES *enters hotel room.*)

CINDY: Maybe some other time—

JAMES *(To* FREDDIE): Excuse me, sir.

FREDDIE *(Noticing* JAMES; *quickly to* CINDY): Can you hold on a second? Someone just came in.

CINDY *(Firmly):* No listen. I really do have to go.

FREDDIE *(Anxiously):* Are you going to be there tomorrow? Seven o'clock? *(Feebly joking)* I'll be the one on the white horse.

CINDY: I don't know. I'll think it over.

FREDDIE *(Insistently):* Well, will you give me your number? I'll call you right back.

CINDY: No, that's all right. I'll call you.

FREDDIE: Then maybe—

CINDY *(Quickly):* Goodbye! *(Hangs up, sighs, looks once more at classifieds, then gets up, crosses room and starts to water plants. FREDDIE, shocked, hangs up. JAMES clears his throat.)*

JAMES: Ah, sir.

FREDDIE *(Turning to face JAMES):* Yes, James?

JAMES: Forgive the interruption, Count Frederick, but your Uncle Roger has taken a turn for the worse. You must return to the palace at once. *(FREDDIE slowly looks back at telephone; JAMES continues.)* They're fueling the plane . . . if you're ready to go now. *(FREDDIE remains silent.)* Count Frederick?

FREDDIE *(Without looking at JAMES):* Yes?

JAMES: Is something wrong, sir?

FREDDIE *(Shaking his head in disbelief):* I didn't even get her first name . . .

CINDY *(Pausing a moment in her watering):* Funny—I didn't even ask him his name . . . *(Quick curtain)*

THE END

PRODUCTION NOTES

DESPERATELY SEEKING PRINCESS

Characters: 2 male; 1 female.

Playing Time: 20 minutes.

Costumes: Freddie wears slacks, oxford shirt, navy blazer. Cindy wears casual clothes and a watch.

Properties: Grocery bag containing sodas and bag of potato chips, teacup, newspaper.

Setting: Split set: At right is Freddie's elegant hotel room in downtown San Francisco. A telephone and vase of fresh roses are on coffee table, which has two chairs behind it. There is a stereo at far right. At left is Cindy's modest apartment, with single chair, and a small table with a telephone and teacup on it; a larger table has potted plants, watering can, hairbrush and nail file on it.

Sound Effects: Phone ringing.